DATE DUE

APR 2 8 1995	
NOV 2 2 1999	
JAN 1 2000	

ONTARIO ARCHITECTURE

ONTARIO ARCHITECTURE

A Guide to Styles and Building Terms
1784 to the Present

John Blumenson

Fitzhenry & Whiteside

<u>Ontario Architecture</u>

© Copyright 1990 Fitzhenry & Whiteside

Editors: Beverly Sotolov-Anderson
        Frank English
Photographs: John Blumenson
Designer: McCalla Design Associates
Typesetter: Isis Communications Limited
Printed and bound in Canada
by T. H. Best Printing Company

Canadian Cataloguing in Publication Data

Blumenson, John J.G., 1942-
   Ontario architecture: a guide to styles and building
   terms (1784-1984)

Bibiliography: p. 251
Includes index.
ISBN 0-88902-872-9

1. Architecture – Ontario. 2. Architecture –
Ontario – Terminology. I Title.

NA746.05B58 1989   720'. 9713   C89-094700-7

Contents

To my loving and generous parents,
Geve and Martin Blumenson

Acknowledgements

Of the many persons who have contributed to this book, my sincerest appreciation and gratitude is extended to three individuals: Mr. Anthony Adamson, architect, historian and author; Dr. Harold Kalman, President, Commonwealth Historic Resources Management Ltd.; and Dr. Thomas McIlwraith, Professor of Geography, University of Toronto. Their early encouragement and support in my endeavour was instrumental to the development of the initial concept. I am further indebted for their pragmatic criticism and constructive comments which have guided the content selection and stylistic approach chosen for the book. Anthony Adamson has reminded me not to lose quality in my search for objective stylistic categories. I have Harold Kalman to thank for suggesting that objectivity must include the vernacular or eclectic as legitimate expressions, having an equal place in our architectural heritage as do the academic or high-styled buildings. Thomas McIlwraith has kept me on rural roads seeking the farmstead in a province where suburban expansion is quickly making the Ontario farm an endangered species. For their shared thoughts, other insightful comments and their continuing interest, I very much thank each of them.

I also acknowledge the generous support of the Secretary of State, the Canada Council, the Ontario Arts Council and the Ontario Heritage Foundation. Financial grants and stipends from these agencies have permitted me to research, write and photograph hundreds of buildings throughout Ontario. I am grateful to the many persons across the Province for their enthusiasm, hospitality and assistance in introducing me to the architecture of their areas. In particular I would like to thank: Julia Beck – London; Fern Beyer – Grimsby; Heather Broadbent – Caledon; Brad Brownlee – Sarnia; Paul Bullock – Brockville; Aleta Burgess – Markham; Dennis Carter-Edwards – Cornwall; Dennis Castellan – Sudbury; Nina Chapple – Hamilton; Paul Dilse – Toronto; Lynne DiStefano – London; Ken Dougherty – Timmins; Lee Ann Doyle – Sarnia; Averil Farlow – Woodstock; Randy Gloss – Windsor; Bill Greer – Toronto;

Pam Handley – North Bay; Gregory Harris – Windsor; Bruce Hawkins – New Liskeard and Haileybury; Lily Ingliss – Kingston; Martha Ann Kidd – Peterborough; Mrs. William Kosny – Thunder Bay; John Lutman – London; J.A. MacDonald – Thunder Bay; Gordon Maycock – Windsor; Evelyn McClean – Windsor; Mike McGrath – Iroquois Falls; Anne McKillop – London; Robert Mikel – Cobourg; John Miller – Burnside House, Brockville; Mrs. C. Nemis – Sudbury; Carolyn O'Neal – Kirkland Lake; Marianne Park – Woodstock; Peter Philibow – Sudbury; Alana Pierini – Iroquois Falls; John Pratt – Windsor; W. Bill Ross – Thunder Bay; Mrs. Roth – Hamilton; Catherine Smale – Simcoe; Christopher and Christina Tossell – Sault Ste. Marie; and Tom Wood – Fairhaven Way, Ottawa.

I thank the dedicated individuals from the following libraries, agencies and institutions whose cooperation and encouragement aided my research endeavours: Christina Cameron, Janet Wright, Natalie Clerk, Rose-Marie Bray, Michel Audy – Parks Canada; Peter Robinson, Brian Hallet, Douglas McIntyre – Public Archives of Canada; Ken McPherson – Province of Ontario Archives; Allen Suddon and librarians – Fine Arts Department and Baldwin Room, Metropolitan Toronto Reference Library; James E. Page, Keith Richardson, Natalie Fenus – Canadian Studies Directorate, Secretary of State; Helen Eriks, Paul Savoie – Explorations Program, Canada Council; Richard Moorhouse, Dan Schneider, Lorne St. Croix – Ontario Heritage Foundation; Valerie Frith – Ontario Arts Council; and Prudence Tracey – University of Toronto.

I also thank Sally Downing at Format Studios for the many hours required to produce superb photographic prints.

While Alex Szatmari is unable to share in the physical results of this endeavour, I thank him for his calm, his patience and his insightful understanding during those periods of discouraging circumstances.

And a very personal note of special appreciation is extended to Mary Lou Evans who, while sharing our lives together, has given me the needed emotional support as well as helpful comments and guidance throughout the written and photographic preparation of this book.

Introduction

Architecture is "easily indulged in since buildings occur everywhere, and forms one of the principal sources of interest in all towns and cities" and " is the only fine art open to the inspection of all and interesting to all.;"

– J.C. Loudon, preface to *An Encyclopedia of Cottage, Farm and Villa Architecture…*, London, 1833

Travelling through Ontario reinforces Loudon's observations. Ontario towns, cities and rural areas throughout the Province exhibit a great variety of architectural styles, building forms and different materials. Some buildings are composed to exacting high-style standards one would expect from an architect, and in others an eclectic mixing of parts from many styles is observed. And, very often, unique elements and forms reflect thoroughly local and vernacular influences at work. This book attempts to find the common elements that unite Ontario's architectural styles while at the same time highlighting distinguishing vernacular features and forms.

More than a guide to 200 years of architectural styles, this book identifies building terms and unique building forms or types not necessarily associated with any one particular style. For example, Octagons are given their own chapter in spite of the many add-on styles they exhibit and Victory houses with their New England, Cape Cod form are separated from the Colonial Revival. In order to best illustrate each style, chosen examples have not been restricted to any one type of building; all types are included, from houses to gas stations. Brief historical statements introduce each chapter. Textbook or high-style examples are compared with their vernacular and regional variations from all parts of the province. This book also goes beyond the traditional view that heritage buildings must be old. Included are "modern" twentieth century styles, of which Ontario has an abundance of extraordinary examples. Perhaps with foresight and sensitive planning these "moderns" may avoid becoming an endangered species as has much of our earlier "historical" colonial heritage.

The intention of this book is to identify and illustrate architectural styles and features as they would be seen along any street or rural highway. More often than not, any one building will exhibit a variety of architectural detailing that present more than any one specific architectural style. This mixing of styles or eclecticism make objective categorization confusing and seemingly impossible. Given the large number of buildings constructed during the last century's "Battle of Styles", this stylistic eclecticism in fact adds immensely to Ontario's architectural richness and it should not be surprising to find this trait continuing to the present day. The word "vernacular" does not mean buildings of a purely functional nature, void of stylistic

1

elements, but buildings that exhibit unique regional or local design characteristics, while at the same time aspiring, however minimal, to high-style architecture. Building materials employed and proportion of compositional parts also help to date construction and distinguish style.

This façade orientation of this book is not presented as a complete history explaining why and how architectural styles have come to be. Those larger questions are best answered in a more comprehensive text. To introduce the reader, style is simply defined as buildings sharing common design characteristics of structure, form and detail. The recognition of these stylistic features, building forms and their related technical terms is but a first step toward an appreciation and awareness of Ontario's architectural heritage.

It should be pointed out that, with this publication about style, it is not the author's intention to over-emphasize the importance of style. When assessing the historical importance of a building or group of buildings, style is but one component or factor in determining its heritage value. Often style assumes a secondary role to other factors, including historical and contextual among many others. It is hoped this guide will become another resource in the architectural conservationist's library.

One factor that prompted the writing of this book was the need to fill a gap in existing literature about Ontario's architectural heritage. There has been a growing interest in , and concern for heritage buildings since the enactment of the Ontario Heritage Act. (1974). Many local heritage advisory boards have been formed, numerous meetings and conferences have been held, hundreds of buildings restored and adapted to new uses and a number of well-researched and and informative publications have appeared. But to date, there has been no publication devoted to succinctly identifying and profusely illustrating architectural styles and their asociated features. No text has exclusively concerned itself with the stylistic grammar and technical terminology of Ontario's architecture from its earliest colonial days to the present.

Settlement patterns, family history and built-form are all important factors when considering the complete value. These two houses, one with Neo-classical and the other with Gothic influences, illustrate how succeeding generations respected the architecture of their ancestors. (near Troy)

The overview provided in this book allows comparisons of architectural styles and elements from all corners of the Province, from Cornwall to Thunder Bay and Sudbury to Leamington.

The highly visual aspect of this book is designed to enable the readers to examine illustrated styles and terms as they would buildings on the street. Therefore, high-profile public buildings have been excluded in favour of less-well-known examples and no interior views are included. For instance, the Provincial Parliament Buildings in Toronto, representative of the Romanesque Revival style, are not illustrated; instead, lesser known but equally representative buildings of that style are used. Several additional photographs illustrate regional variations and vernacular interpretations with brief captions highlighting unique elements. A brief statement that precedes each chapter, places the style in an Ontario context and outlines the general characteristics of that style. For the reader wishing to know more, a bibliography is included. A cross-referenced index has been included, directing the reader to both stylistic and technical terms found throughout the book. A more detailed illustrated glossary of building terms is in preparation for later publication.

This book is presented with the hope that the readers, once having sampled the grammar and vocabulary of Ontario's rich and varied architectural heritage, will endeavour to look and learn about buildings in their immediate area. This book is meant to be read, looked at, and then applied in the field. When conducting field trips, the user is requested to respect the privacy of the occupants of not only the illustrated buildings, but all private residences that may attract their attention. To this end, properties illustrated in this book are located only by the county, city of town.

Preparation for this book required many hours of research and reading: from eighteenth century treatises to twentieth century architectural journals. With further research and analysis, descriptions of styles and terms may be refined requiring this guide to be updated. While many persons assisted in gathering information, any errors of fact or interpretation are my sole responsibility. For general stylistic nomenclature, I have relied heavily on existing guide books, both North American and European, including my previous publication *Identifying American Architecture*. It also entailed photographic treks across the Province on rainy, snowy and (fortunately) sunny days with deep blue skies. The reception by many members of historical groups, heritage advisory boards, municipal employees, architects and concerned private citizens have been welcome and fruitful experiences. The interest and support shown by individual property owners was particularly surprising and very much appreciated.

Chapter 1 Georgian (1784-1860)

Holland Landing

While Georgian refers to the soverign rule of the Georges, in architectural terms Georgian generally refers to the continuation of the English Renaissance and Palladian Classicism as practised in both England and the colonies during the eighteenth century. Buildings in the Georgian style are characterized by uncluttered designs based on an adherence to conventional rules of symmetry and proportion. House façades are formally arranged with an equal balance of parts (doors and windows) on either side of a central motif (the frontispiece or entrance) and accentuated with a select distribution of Classical embellishments, including roof and window cornices, moulded surrounds and a small entrance portico. The resulting balanced harmony outlined with Classical details was in sharp contrast to the older informal and rambling multishaped medieval houses of pre-Renaissance England.

In Ontario the Georgian style was brought to the Province of Upper Canada late in the Georgian period by the English and by the United Empire Loyalists, refugees from the American War of Independence. Due to the severe climate, the harshness of the land and in particular the limited financial resources of these early settlers, their buildings, with few exceptions, evidence structural necessity more than academic stylistic features, as was the case in the United States or England. Given the varied backgrounds of these settlers, what they built often imparted vernacular methods of construction reflecting their origins, skills and, when possible, their personal aesthetics. There were few substantial buildings constructed in the opening decades of settlement in Upper Canada, and those that have survived have invariably been added to, modernized or otherwise altered during the past two hundred years of development. After the War of 1812, and with the arrival of more and more people to the Province, Neoclassical and Regency influences quickly modernized the Georgian frame. Many early Georgian-style buildings, both high style and vernacular, were either completely rebuilt or remodelled according to the latest fashions from London, New York or far-away India. However, Georgian symmetry, order and formality remained prominent characteristics of Ontario architecture for many years. The style was so popular, in fact, that mid-nineteenth century houses possessing strong eighteenth century Georgian traits are often labelled Late Georgian, or Georgian Survival.

Georgian (1784-1860)

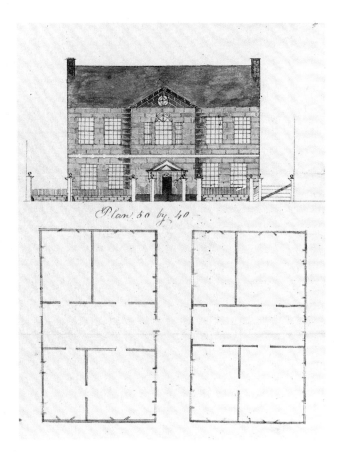

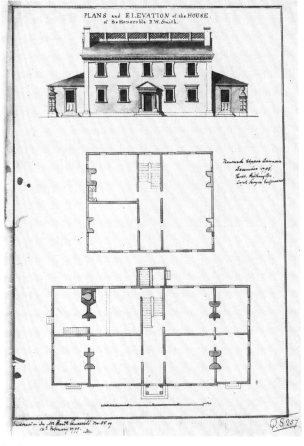

1−1
William Dickson House, ca. 1794, Niagara-on-the-Lake
Noteworthy features include:
- *steep roof slope with large chimneys*
- *ashlar or cut stone walls*
- *projecting pedimented frontispiece*
- *round or circular light or ventilator in pediment*
- *Palladian window*
- *twelve-over-twelve light sash-type windows*
- *continuous string or belt course*
- *half-round fanlight over the door*
- *indication of pedimented portico or other embellishment*

1−2
D. W. Smith House, ca. 1794, Niagara-on-the-Lake
Noteworthy features include:
- *large chimneys on the slope, probably linked to another on the rear slope*
- *balustraded roof railing and possible deck*
- *moulded cornice with modillion blocks*
- *monumental corner pilasters or piers*
- *window cornice*
- *shouldered architrave window surrounds*
- *pedimented portico with Ionic columns*
- *symmetrically opposed or balanced wings with banded gateposts*

The D.W. Smith House and the William Dickson House, both destroyed in 1813, are fine representatives of a well-to-do Englishman's Georgian colonial home. They display an orderly façade of symmetrically balanced parts with Classical detailing. The Dickson House (see 1−1) is distinguished by a projecting frontispiece highlighted by a three-part window known as a Palladian motif. The Smith House (see 1−2) is marked by a Classical roof railing, cornice with modillion blocks, moulded window surrounds and a bold pedimented portico. The lack of sidelights flanking the entrance should be noted; the door in the Dickson House is topped with a small half-round fanlight.

1-3
This vernacular stone building is highlighted with academic-inspired Georgian door surround including fluted pilasters and a denticulated pediment. (Maitland)

1-4
With the exception of the wide Neoclassical entrance, the form of this house is very similar to the eighteenth century William Dickson House (see 1-1). The elliptical fanlight of the Neoclassical style incorporated the entire door and flanking sidelights. (Kingston)

Georgian (1784-1860)

Characteristic of the vernacular Georgian constructed by the Loyalist is the plain brick or timber-frame house of generous proportions, with large chimneys and a minimal amount, if any, of Classical detailing. An example is the house in Mallorytown (see 1–6), which in spite of its changes in roofing material and window glazing retains the proportions and building materials typical of the close of the eighteenth century. Noteworthy are the flemish bond brick walls, the overdoor fanlight, steep roof, large chimneys and, of course, the formal arrangement of apertures in relation to the walls. Another property, restored as a museum along the Niagara Parkway, is the MacFarland House (see 1–5), which shares with the Mallorytown example the proportions, the flemish bond brick walls and the flat or jack arched window heads. The twelve-over-twelve light sash-type windows are also typical, as are the louvered shutters, though solid wood panel shutters were often used. The MacFarland House differs in its straight transom overdoor light. The lower pitch roof indicates a possible change to the roofline or a date of construction sometime after 1813.

1–5

While high-style decorative motifs are not evident on the exterior of this house, Georgian Classical traditions are reflected in the formal centre hall, symmetrical composition of the windows and door openings, as well as eighteenth century building techniques such as flemish bond brickwork and the narrow transom light over the door. In addition, it has a generous amount of wall space in relation to the size of the windows. (The MacFarland House, Niagara Parkway)

1-6
Georgian features of this simple but well-proportioned five-bay house include large end-wall chimneys, steep gable roof and half-round fanlight over the door. (Mallorytown)

1-7
This interpretation of Georgian stylistic principles is executed with vernacular rough-cut rubble-stone walls that provide a frame for a symmetrical distribution of openings centred on an entrance with large, but not full-length sidelights. Note, also, that the transom light is only as wide as the door, not the complete entrance. The shallow-pitched hip roof adds a very modern or Regency-style flair to the overall composition. (The Ermatinger House, Sault Ste. Marie)

1—8
The thick stone walls of this substantial house provide space for deep-panelled reveals for the arched entrance. The medium-pitched gable roof with quarter-round lights or attic ventilators is more characteristic of the nineteenth century than the eighteenth. (Burritt's Rapids)

1—9
Beneath several dominant nineteenth century additions lies the basic five-bay, one-and-a-half-storey- vernacular frame house built by Loyalist refugees during the 1790s and 1800s. Noteworthy features include the small-paned twelve-over-twelve light sash-type windows, the centre door flanked by separate sidelights and the large chimney with an exposed brick base along the end wall. The centre gable and room over the porch were probably added toward the end of the nineteenth century. (Carrying Place)

1–10
The generous amount of wall space relative to the small window openings and the steep roof slope punctuated with large chimneys indicate early vernacular building characteristics, while the exceptionally wide entry with full transom light is a feature more popular with the Neoclassical style of the 1820s. (Sandwich)

1–11
If constructed in brick, this building would appear not much different from a Georgian double house of eighteenth century Boston or London. Note the large chimneys, the flat stone arch over each opening, the simple but moulded window surrounds, solid wood-panelled shutters and entrance doors with small transom light. (Kingston)

1—12

1—13

Many early nineteenth century vernacular houses maintained Georgian symmetry with small multipaned sash windows, flat or jack arched window heads and flemish bond brick walls (1—12, Portsmouth), while others incorporated up-to-date refinements, such as delicate curvilinear tracery in sidelights and transom lights surrounding the door or an awning-profiled veranda, features more familiar to the Neoclassical and Regency styles. (1—13, Bond Head)

Chapter 2 Neoclassical (1800-1860)

Toronto

In comparison with the Georgian style, the Neoclassical is characterized by a more refined and lighter version of Classical architecture. The Neoclassical selected and reinterpretated past forms and features with greater latitude and freedom. The Georgian concerned itself with Roman architecture secondhand, as interpreted by Renaissance architects, while the Neoclassical looked directly to antiquity; the archaeological discoveries of Imperial Rome during the second half of the eighteenth century were the inspiration for renewed study and emulation, not copying.

One of the most influential British architects of this period was Robert Adam (1728-1792), who led the way in adapting Roman architectural orders, forms and decorative motifs. He was aided by his brother James, and the two were so successful that this style is often referred to as the Adam style. Their most important publication, based on observations, sketches and drawings made during and after personal examinations of Roman sites, *Works in Architecture*, appeared in three volumes: 1773, 1779 and 1822. In America, the Neoclassical style was promoted by Asher Benjamin and others in numerous handbooks, the earliest being *The Country Builder's Assistant*, published in Boston in 1798. The style is known there today as Federal. Stylized Classical elements, such as columns, pilasters and mouldings are thin in proportion, appearing elongated or attenuated, and the spacing between columns is often not in strict accordance with academic prototypes. Façades are highlighted with arcades, monumental pilaster strips, decorative friezes, large windows and generously wide entrances ideally having an elliptical profile. When the transom is not arched but rectangular, the tracery bars radiate, aspiring to form an arch of fanlike shape. The tracery bars of the sidelights often take on intricate lacelike patterns. Windows are multipaned sash types similar to the Georgian style; however, the individual lights or panes are fewer in number, and the apertures or openings are larger in size. Sidelights may flank a central window in a variation of the Palladian motif known as a Venetian window. Bow windows indicating oval or round interior rooms are an innovative feature of the Neoclassical style.

Neoclassical (1800-1860)

In Ontario the symmetry and formality of the Georgian continued to play an important part in the overall composition. And it is very common to find traditional Georgian elements, both vernacular and high style, directly adopted as well as adapted to suit Neoclassical tastes. The chief distinguishing feature of the Ontario Neoclassical is the wide entrance framed by fluted pilasters, sidelights and a generous transom light ideally having an elliptical profile that stretches across both the door and sidelights. In many cases the structurally more difficult arched light was omitted in favour of the straight transom. Generally, façades have larger window apertures and wider entrances than Georgian examples. Roofs usually gabled tend not to be as steep, but chimneys remain dominant along the ridge at both gable ends. Decorative friezes along the roof cornice are popular, as are short cornice returns at each corner. It is common to find a small pedimented portico or porch supported by coupled columns of thin diameter. Houses of modest proportions may omit the elliptical fanlight in favour of the straight transom with a solid-board entablature with a wide frieze that may be decorated with garlands or festoons. On more pretentious academic-inspired buildings, when the projecting frontispiece is applied, it is less pronounced than in the Georgian style. Quarter-round and half-round lunette-shaped apertures continue to decorate gable ends and pediments, but are commonly glazed to provide light.

2–1

The Campbell House, 1822, Toronto. Noteworthy features of this high-style Neoclassical house include:
- *shallow and wide projecting frontispiece with pediment*
- *elliptical fanlight*
- *half-round portico*
- *tall windows with thin muntins or glazing bars*
- *oval light*
- *moulded cornice with returns*

Representative of the academic or high-style version of the Neoclassical is the Campbell House (1822) in Toronto (see 2–1). Constructed in flemish bond brick, the house is highlighted with a projecting frontispiece shallower than its Georgian predecessor and also wider, incorporating three of the façade's five bays, thus enabling the crowning pediment to assume a Classical profile. Also characteristic is the wide double-door entrance and spacious, elliptical-fanlight transom embracing the door plus sidelights. Other academic features include the rounded portico, large windows with thin muntins or glazing bars and the elongated oval window in the pediment.

A vernacular application of Neoclassical elements combined with very traditional eighteenth century characteristics is seen in the timber-frame clapboarded Macpherson House (ca. 1820-30) in Napanee. Traits inherited from the Georgian style of the previous century include the symmetrical balance of windows around the central entrance, small multipaned sash-type windows, large chimneys and the dormer placed close to the roof eaves. The placement of the kitchen wing against an end wall is a typical building practice when the centre through-hall plan is used. A very common Neoclassical treatment is seen in the entrance, where within the confines of the rectangular transom the glazing bars radiate, imitating the desired high-style elliptical-fanlight motif. This curvilinear theme is varied in the sidelights and in the upper-floor, three-part Venetian window. Multiple mouldings with corner blocks framing the entrance and the cornice returns also aspire to high-style precedent. The thin pilaster strips flanking the doorway appear incomplete, suggesting the possible prior existence of a portico.

2–2
The Macpherson House (ca. 1820-30), Napanee. Noteworthy features of this transitional Neoclassical vernacular house include:
- *wide rectangular transom light with glazing bars radiating in fanlike form*
- *lacelike glazing bars*
- *Venetian window*
- *cornice returns with multiple mouldings*
- *beaded corner boards*
- *simple window frames with plain drip-board cornice*

Neoclassical (1800-1860)

2–3
Where a glass transom was not practical, the fan motif was carved in wood and framed with fluted pilasters and a denticulated cornice. (Bath)

2–4
This vernacular timber-frame building is distinguished by a formal arrangement of thin pilaster strips supporting a cornice enriched with a series of fanlike motifs that is repeated above the pilaster-enframed entrance. (Bath)

2–5
This simple frame dwelling characterized by its vernacular salt-box form is highlighted by a single aspiration to style, the door surround with thin pilasters and shelflike projecting cornice. (The Bradley House, Clarkson, Mississauga)

2-6
The vernacular interpretation of the academic Neoclassical doorway is marked by sidelights separated by pilasters supporting a full three-part entablature consisting of a narrow architrave, plain but generously wide frieze and a thin projecting cornice. (Churchville)

2-7
This simple vernacular wood-clad house aspires to stylistic pretention with pilasters and full entablatures framing not only the entrance but the windows, as well. (Moira)

2-8
This modest but formidable Georgian house frame is marked with small-paned sash windows and a wide Neoclassical arched fanlight entrance. (Maitland)

2–9
The similar house form, as seen in the Campbell House (see 2–1), is modified in stone while retaining the smaller windows more typical of the earlier century and the Georgian style. (The Matheson House, Perth)

2–10
The favoured elliptical arch is used here for the entrance as well as for the lunette in the open pediment. The arched theme is carried further with the curved tracery bars. (Cardinal)

2–11
A late vernacular interpretation of the Neoclassical fanlight entrance survives with Gothic elements. The shallow pitch of the centre gable belongs more to earlier Classical traditions than to the acutely pointed centre gable of the Gothic Revival style. (Pittsburgh Township)

2–12
Lightness of detail is evident in the attenuated pilaster strips, thin muntin bars and shallow mouldings of these arched church windows. (Williamstown)

Chapter 3 # Regency (1830-60)

Odessa

As an architectural style, the Regency began in England in 1815, when the Prince Regent engaged the architect John Nash to build the Royal Pavilion at Brighton as an exotic version of an Indian temple. In Ontario the Regency arrived several years later, when retiring British officers came to Canada and wished to emulate the Prince Regent in recalling distant places where they had served the King. Unable to allow themselves Indian temples or palaces, they settled for dwellings with less costly romantic allusions. In comparison with the Loyalist who brought to Ontario eighteenth century English traditions acquired in the American colonies, the officer and immigrating British merchant alike brought the latest fashions from London as well as remembrances from all parts of the Empire.

Recalling the more tropical climates of the Far East and Mediterranean rather than considering the severe Canadian winter, the officer added a long veranda with canopylike roof extending the length of the house and generous floor-to-ceiling windows, sometimes doubling as doors, known as French doors. The veranda, often with trellislike supports, combined with a modest one-storey rectangular house covered with a gently pitched hip roof are characteristic of the Ontario Regency cottage. For the Regency architect or builder, "cottage" never meant a seasonal or temporary home, but a properly built house for year-round living. A more commodious two-storey "villa" was built for those with the means and need for additional rooms. In either case, cottage or villa, the preferred exterior finish was stucco, sometimes scored to imitate cut stone. In order to maintain the low "cottage" profile, second-floor windows were often smaller than those on the ground floor, at times approaching a square outline. Similar windows can also be seen on some Classic Revival houses.

During the early nineteenth century the picturesque began to play an important role in the design and orientation of the house. Sacrificing practical considerations of wind direction or snow, the Regency cottage or villa preferred a geographically advantageous view. The view to and from the house was of utmost importance. Landscape improvements and auxiliary buildings, such as a garden gazebo and dovecote, or pigeon house, were also considered integral to the overall picturesqueness of the property. The resulting Regency-style house, often symmetrical in the Georgian or Classical traditions, is frequently highlighted with features romantically inspired from more ancient times and faraway places. For example, this romantic appeal may reveal itself in the discriminating use of a Gothic window, a Greek moulding or an Italian cornice. This selective mixing of a Classical frame with elements from divergent stylistic origins marks the beginning of eclecticism in Ontario architecture, a characteristic trait visible on many houses today. Later nineteenth and twentieth century interpretations of the Regency cottage, either characterized by a variety of additive stylistic features or just as often by a lack of them, became so widespread throughout Canada and so representative of this province that all hipped-roof one-storey houses were often labelled the Ontario Regency cottage.

Regency features existing side by side with Neoclassical elements are well-llustrated in the Robinson-Adamson House (ca. 1835) Erindale (see 3 1). The typical Regency one storey hip roof form with generous fenestration and wide entry is highlighted by an elegant Neoclassical-inspired frieze, door and window enframements. The Venetian or three-part window configuration is framed

3–1
The Ontario Regency cottage form is combined with high-style Neoclassical decorative mouldings and fenestration into a unique academic exercise resulting in more glass than wall. (Robinson-Adamson House, ca. 1835, Erindale, Mississauga)
Noteworthy features include:
– paired tall chimneys on slope of roof
– large windows divided by thin glazing bars into a variety of square and rectangular panes
– hip roof with shallow pitch

with pilasterlike mouldings supporting a full entablature with a pronounced projecting cornice. More akin to the Regency is the arrangement of the thin muntins or glazing bars dividing the tall casement windows, the transom and the sidelights of the entry into a series of squares and narrow rectangles. While this pattern heightens the simple boxlike composition of the house, it is lightened by the elegant frieze consisting of a series of suspended elliptical arches. The pair of chimneys to the right are mirrored by another pair on the opposing slope. The dormers are probably of a recent date and necessary to light the upper floor. There is no evidence to indicate the existence of a veranda. This omission and the Neoclassical influences are more readily understood from the fact that the first owner of the cottage was of Loyalist background.

More typical of the vernacular Ontario Regency cottage is the modest brick house in Bowmanville (see 3–2), whose veranda exhibits decorative detailing characteristic of later nineteenth century styles, such as the Queen Anne. However, the one-storey, shallow-pitched hip-roof form combined with wide entry and tall paired windows is in the best tradition of the Regency cottage. The placement and thin dimension of the chimney indicate a reliance on a single stove or furnace rather than multiple chimneys and stoves, as would have been required earlier in the century.

3–2
The characteristic one-storey hipped-roof cottage with tall first-floor French doors is highlighted by a full-length veranda with fanciful late-nineteenth-century wood detailing. (Bowmanville)
Noteworthy features include:
– shallow-pitched hip roof
– French doors
– full-length veranda
– unadorned cornice

3–3
Reminiscent of the Classic Revival, Greek Doric pilasters frame the entrance and solid lintels span the French doors in this Regency-cottage form adapted to stone. (Dundas)

3–4
The Regency villa form mixed with Neoclassical preferences for rounded forms and attenuated Classical features is evidenced in the bowed bays and entrance portico. The narrow transom and separate sidelights of the main door denote traditional Georgian elements. (Cobourg)

3–5
The horizontality of the main house, based upon Georgian rules of formal symmetry, is enhanced by the low roofline, the deep roof eaves, the small cubelike second-floor windows and the flanking lateral wings. These compositional attributes together with landscape features create the desired picturesqueness of a gentleman's rural estate. (Sibbald Manor, ca. 1835-40, Jackson's Point)

3–6
The Regency's preference for selected fanciful detailing is seen in this adoption of Neoclassical tracery in the rectilinear transom and sidelights, where the glazing bars interlace to form elliptical, half-round and diamond patterns. (Main entrance to Sibbald Manor, ca. 1835-40, Jackson's Point)

3–7
A Gothic accent in the form of a lancet window adds diversity to this informal villa. (Cobourg)

3–8
The length of this three-bay cottage is heightened by the self-supporting projecting eaves of the exaggerated hip roof, creating an umbrage nearly equal to a veranda. (Colborne)

3-9
In spite of a centre gable and numerous changes, including the conversion from single to double house, the overall shape and tall first-floor French doors reveal the existence of a Regency cottage beneath the vinyl siding. (Streetsville, Mississauga)

3-10
The Regency cottage form is brought up to date with late twentieth century materials and details. (Iroquois Falls)

3-11
The ideal expression for a Regency-style veranda assumes a tentlike profile known as an awning roof. Variations of this veranda are also seen on some Gothic Revival houses. (Odessa)

After the Regency, the romantic interest in the ancient and picturesque quickly developed into separate stylistic modes. Architects and their clients began to copy temples, ancient buildings and monuments in total. In particular the Classic and the Gothic Revivals became widely accepted in Ontario. It should not be forgotten that the founding architect of the Regency's eclectic romanticism, John Nash, was as comfortable designing in the Indian style as in the Gothic or Classic. But the Regency's interest in the ancient, the antique and the exotic was primarily in fantasy, not the academic or scholastic, as developed by the next generation.

Chapter 4

Classic Revival (1830-1860)

Merrickville

As early as 1762, a serious interest in Greek architecture of the fifth century B.C. was evidenced by the publication of Stuart and Revett's *Antiquities of Athens*. A total of four volumes had appeared by 1816, with a supplementary one in 1830. In addition to the architecture of Imperial Rome, also recently rediscovered and embodied in the Neoclassical style, the architects of eighteenth century England now had the vocabulary of Greek architecture at their disposal. By 1800, Classic influences, both Roman and Greek, were evident in the works of such English architects as Soane and Nash. And Grecian elements were popular in Regency-style houses.

By the 1830s in Ontario and the United States, this interest in Classic architecture developed into a true revival. So popular and widespread was the interest in Greek forms that the style has been referred to as the Greek Revival. Numerous pattern books were published, outlining the Classic architectural orders and providing how-to advice on construction and finish, including modifying or improving the temple form to modern uses. A sampling of such books includes Asher Benjamin's earliest work, *The Country Builder's Assistant*, of 1798; his popular *American Builder's Companion*, with editions from 1806-55; Minard Lefever's *The Modern Builder's Guide*, with editions from 1833-55; as well as scores of other titles.

Classic architecture can be broadly defined as that of ancient Greece and Rome. The Greeks developed three architectural orders: the Doric, the Ionic and the Corinthian. The Romans subsequently modified these basic three, adding the Tuscan and the more elaborate Composite. Each of these architectural orders is identifiable by its treatment of the column, including the base, shaft and capital supporting the entablature—from the simplest Tuscan order with minimal mouldings and smooth shafts, to the more elaborate Corinthian with multiple mouldings, fluted shafts and foliated capitals. In addition to their unique ornamentation, each order in theory possessed its own proportional system based upon the diameter of the column. Adherence to these orders depended on the knowledge and skill of the attending architect or

4-1

The Barnum House, Grafton, 1817. Notable features of this transitional temple-plan house include:
- *frieze with metopes and triglyphs*
- *monumental pilasters supporting an arcade of elliptical arches*
- *pedimented roof with tympanum or*
- *pedimented roof facing the front*
- *tympanum with half-round light or lunette*
- *pedimented door surround*
- *blind fanlight*
- *chimneys on cross axis with roof ridge*
- *small-paned sash windows*
- *butt-joined horizontal board siding*

4-2

Former Courthouse, Whitby, 1852, Cumberland and Storm, architects. Notable features of this academic interpretation of a Classic temple front include:
- *columns with fluted shaft resting directly on stylobate or floor*
- *capital with echinus below and abacus above*
- *full entablature with architrave, frieze and cornice*
- *frieze with metopes and triglyphs*
- *raking cornice*
- *tympanum*
- *battered or inclined window jambs with eared upper corners*
- *frieze windows or ventilators*
- *domed lantern with columns in the Ionic order, characterized by volute or scroll-like capitals*

Classic Revival (1830-1860)

builder. The trained English architect was academically well-versed in the Classic orders, while his rural counterpart, the builder or carpenter, relied on his pattern books as a guide, adjusting the rules according to his experience and abilities.

4–3
The temple-plan form adapted to public use and embellished with rustication or stone bonding and cut-stone window surrounds. (Courthouse, Pembroke)

The most striking and popular form of the Classic Revival is the temple form or plan. Often executed in the bold unadorned Doric order, the low-pitch pediment roof is supported by a series of freestanding columns forming a monumental portico. To either side of this façade may be lower one-storey wings. Where the grand portico was undesired, a more modest one-storey version enhanced the entrance. Full-length pilasters framing the corners of the house support a full but plain entablature with wide architrave, frieze and cornice. Typical decorative features include the anthemion or stylized palmette, the fret moulding and the patera or rosette. Windows and doors, invariably of the lintel or straight-headed variety, often have battered or inclined surrounds with eared or shouldered corners. Panelled entrance doors, at times treated with a single vertical panel, are flanked by sidelights framed by pilasters or columns. Multipaned sash-type windows have large individual lights. An upper floor may be lighted by small rectangular windows in the frieze of the entablature covered with a decorative iron grille. Whether built of stone, brick or wood, the preferred exterior finish was smooth and painted white to give the appearance of marble, the material the Greeks used twenty-five hundred years ago.

Since the arch and its related forms, the dome and vault, are associated with Roman architecture, their use with the Greek orders must have been compromising from a purist's point of view. The nineteenth century builder saw no difficulty, for the most part, in placing a dome or arched doorway on a Greek Doric temple. Attempts to copy or recreate exact Roman or Greek temples were rarely realized in practice; they masked every sort of function–houses, banks and churches. To the nineteenth century mind, this incongruity in use and mixture of forms was not considered blasphemous or even eclectic, as the ultimate source was the ancient Classical world.

4–4
A vernacular version of the Classic Revival retains its temple form, large-paned sash windows and vertically panelled door flanked by narrow sidelights. (Niagara)

4–5
This three-unit row or terrace is highlighted with Classic Revival features painted white, including shouldered door surrounds, monumental two-storey pilasters and wide frieze punctuated by small ventilators or grilles. (Port Hope)

4–6

The Ionic order is applied to this portico with columns in antis or between square piers. The scroll-like volutes are supported by tall fluted shafts resting on squared bases with numerous or compound mouldings. The entrance door with small fanlight follows the Georgian tradition established some fifty years earlier. (Seventh Post Office, Toronto, 1851-53, Cumberland and Storm)

4–7

A portico in the Greek Doric order enhances the façade of this centre-hall house of vernacular Georgian inspiration. The linear quality of the cornice is continued in stone across the façade and the vertical fluting of the columns is uniquely imitated in the carved-stone shutters. (Merrickville)

4-8

The bold and austere Doric order was, on occasion, adapted to large institutional or public buildings. In this example, a dramatic three-storey portico and an elongated cupola or lantern highlight the centre, and the flanking wings or pavilions repeat the centre pediment roof profile. (formerly Victoria College, Cobourg, ca. 1832)

4-9

A Classic Revival pediment roof shape is rendered by a bold cornice with returns completed in vernacular fashion with a band of dichromatic brick crosses. (Streetsville, Mississauga)

Classic Revival (1830-1860)

4–10
In spite of the altered entrance, the white-painted straight window cornices and denticulated cornice with returns identify basic Classic Revival features of this vernacular farmhouse. (Mississauga)

4–11
Encircling this one-storey Regency-cottage form is a series of white-painted squared columns supporting a clean entablature in the Doric order. (Hamilton Place, ca. 1844, Paris)

4−12
A vernacular interpretation of the Roman Tuscan order is seen in this temple front with widely spaced smooth columns, a broad pediment with circular light, plain projecting cornice and horizontal boards imitating the finish of a cut-stone or ashlar wall. (Bath)

4−13
Monumental or giant pilasters support a definite Greek-inspired entablature with denticulated cornice. Pedimented window cornices stand in contrast to the Roman-inspired round-arched windows and domed lanternlike bell tower. (Cayuga)

Classic Revival (1830-1860)

4—14
In spite of various changes, including a new exterior surface of rough cast stucco, the temple form remains evident. (Kent County)

4—15
The wide cornice with returns is the prime Classic Revival feature of this vernacular frame house with early twentieth century veranda and enclosed second-floor sun porch. (Colborne)

4—16
This partial temple-plan dwelling is distinguished by an unusually wide entrance, tall first-floor windows and a lunette window in the tympanum of the open pediment. The exceptional cornice is constructed of moulded or contoured bricks painted white, imitating a stone finish. (Cobourg)

Chapter 5 Gothic Revival (1830-1900)

The Gothic Revival style reflects a rekindling of interest in the building forms and styles of the various periods of English Gothic, as well as the years preceding the English Renaissance, i.e., the Tudor and Elizabethan periods. Thus we see in Ontario a great variety of features, forms and building elements from differing Gothic and/or medieval periods at times used simultaneously on the same building.

In the area of domestic building, A. J. Downing, the American landscape architect, in such publications as *Cottage Residences*, 1840, and his contemporary English mentor, J. C. Loudon, in his *Encyclopaedia*, 1833, provided aesthetic theory, plans and elevations and practical hints for the construction of all sizes and manner of dwelling in various Gothic and Medieval styles. Their proposed designs tended to the picturesque in composition and the eclectic in their selection of architectural detail. In Ontario some early Gothic Revival buildings may share a similar overall form with the classical Georgian and Neoclassical styles and are distinguished solely by their "add on" Gothic details. The most common and often singular feature shared by many houses across the Province is the simple lancet or pointed window, located in the centre gable above the main door. Another common detail is the vergeboard or bargeboard, a roof trim ideally decorated with curvilinear patterns. Hood-moulds with carved label stops, numerous dormers and gables, finials, pinnacles and crockets are other features highlighting a formal brick villa or modest frame dwelling. Bay windows, verandas and a steep roof pierced by tall decorated chimney stacks also add to the ideal picturesque quality of the building. Timber-frame buildings were often finished with vertical boards and battens, a method highly recommended by Downing.

A strict academic approach to interpreting Gothic architecture was professed by the English architect and critic A. Pugin. In such books as *The True Principles of Pointed or Christian Architecture*, 1841, he advocated a more direct and correct application of English Gothic architecture in opposition to the then practice of simply applying Gothic details to a Classical frame. His views were

Gothic Revival (1830-1900)

supported in religious architecture by the Cambridge Camden Society, which provided architectural advice to its Anglican parishes throughout the British Empire. Generally, historical prototypes tended to be selected from the early English and decorated periods of Gothic architecture. Thus by the mid-nineteenth century many Ontario churches tended to be, if not archaeologically correct, at least academically appropriate, while a greater individual expression was permitted in the design of houses.

5–1
Noteworthy features on this early Gothic Revival example (Elizabeth Cottage, ca. 1841-43, Kingston) include:
- *pointed hood-mould*
- *depressed-arch hood-mould*
- *castellated cornice*
- *trefoil moulding*
- *curvilinear vergeboards*
- *floriated label stop*
- *finial*

5–2
While Classical in symmetrical composition, this commodious centre-hall house achieves a Gothic image with corbel-stepped gables, stone finials and an encircling veranda highlighted with Tudor arches. Other noteworthy typical details include stone corbels, straight hood-moulds with label stops and casement-type windows. (Grosvenor Lodge, London, 1853)

5–3

The castellated version with battlemented parapets, towers, narrow windows, not always pointed, and smooth monochromatic exterior finishes was popular for early Gothic Revival public buildings. (Middlesex County Courthouse, London, 1827-31, with later additions, John Ewart, architect)

5–4

The hallmark of Gothic Revival architecture, the simple pointed lancet window is given a Regency interpretation with multipane windows and thin muntin bars. (L'Orignal)

5-5

5-6

The projecting porch with chamber above is less a variation of the Classical frontispiece than a vestige of the Medieval box-hall plan. (5-5, Erin; 5-6, Streetsville)

5-7

Small Gothic Revival cottages were promoted by such academics as J. C. Loudon and A. J. Downing, but also by The Canada Farmer *in 1865, identifying it simply as "a cheap country dwelling house". (*The Canada Farmer, *vol. II, 1865, p.244). Vernacular variations of this small centre-gable cottage were very popular with plain brick (5-8, Markham) or with dichromatic brick accents (5-9, Brampton; 5-10, Uxbridge) or with an awning or tent-shaped veranda reflecting Regency-style aspirations. (5-11, Watford)*

5-8

5-10

5-9

5-11

Gothic Revival (1830-1900)

Dichromatic brick patterns, gables and dormers, various window shapes and sizes, mixed vergeboards and verandas are all typical features seen on a multitude of L-shaped Victorian Gothic dwellings in many parts of the province dating from the nineteenth century and well into the twentieth century. (5-12, Brighton; 5-13, Kingston; 5-14, St. George; 5-15 Nobleton; 5-16 Pembrooke; 5-17 Uxbridge)

5-12

5-13

5-14

5–15

5–16

5–17

Gothic Revival (1830-1900)

After 1850 a shift in the repertoire of the Gothic Revival occurred, which is appropriately labelled Victorian Gothic. This version of the Gothic Revival was ushered onto the scene primarily by the English philosopher and critic J. Ruskin, who differed from his contemporaries by promoting the picturesque and decorative qualities inherent in the architecture not only of England but, most important, the Gothic of other parts of central and southern Europe. In *Seven Lamps of Architecture*, 1849, and in the *Stones of Venice*, 1850, he admired the highly colouristic façades of the Venetian Gothic as well as the structural qualities of Medieval building techniques. After Ruskin, inspiration from a variety of Gothic styles with emphasis on structure and polychromy became the rule, and their diversified and eclectic application led to occasional distortion or exaggeration of elements.

In Ontario evidence of this change was often seen in vergeboards and other wooden trim along gables, dormers and porches. Vergeboards often have more than one decorative pattern. Rather than the open, lacelike trim flowing from gable to gable, multiple geometric and foliated patterns are mixed and often change from gable to gable. A more direct approach to expressing structure is evidenced when vergeboards imitate roof-framing members; e.g., king posts, cross beams, purlins and rafters are assembled on the exterior of the gables and dormers in much the same manner as real roof framing. Additionally, a secondary lighter decorative pattern is often inserted between the primary larger framelike members. While the pointed-arch window remains a distinguishing

5—18
A strong sense of varied materials, each possessing a unique colour or texture and arranged in complex and at times exaggerated compositions, hallmark the academic version of the Victorian Gothic style. (Knox College, Toronto, 1875, Smith and Gemmell, architects)

feature, a mixture of openings, including the segmental arch, becomes more and more popular, and even a round-headed window may be used. For the most part, sash windows have two-over-two lights. By 1900 it was common to see narrow one-over-one-light sash windows grouped together in a single large opening.

The hallmark of Gothic Revival architecture, the simple pointed lancet window, is given two distinct vernacular applications as seen in the pronounced hood-moulds of academic origins (5−19, Holland Landing) and the exaggerated polychromy of the vernacular (5−20, Morrisburg).

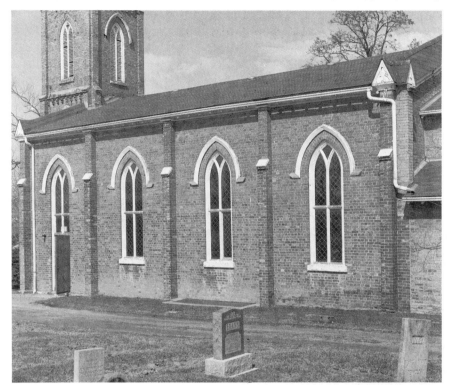

5−19

5−20

5-21

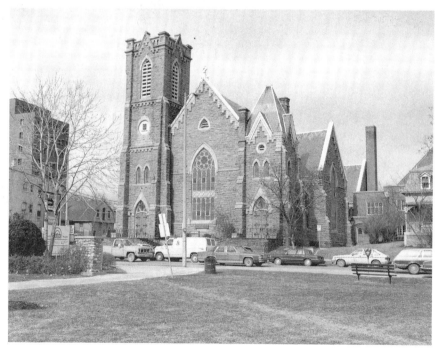

5-22

Victorian Gothic churches differ from their earlier versions by a more complicated floorplan and overall asymmetrical elevation with details freely drawn from a variety of Medieval sources or prototypes. (5—21, Thunder Bay; 5—22, Brampton; 5—23, Brantford)

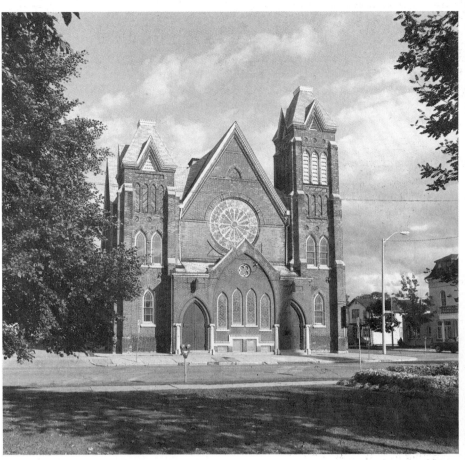

5–23

The use of two tones of brick, usually red brick highlighted with buff or yellow bricks, known as dichromatic brickwork, a popular feature seen on many rural houses and churches, is a vernacular attempt at achieving the polychromatic effects described by Ruskin. Such polychromatic effects are more striking in public and civic examples, where the architect was allowed greater latitude in design and liberty in selecting materials. A single building may be composed of several materials each having its own distinctive colour: i.e., granite, marble, sandstone and terra cotta. Architectural details such as string courses, mouldings and surrounds in contrasting colours may accentuate windows, doors and arches. The roof, generally steep with cross gables, dormers and finials, may be outlined with oversized towers or turrets, creating a top-heavy or awkward balance. Iron roof cresting is also popular in this style.

In church design, the picturesque steep gable roof is given an added vertical dimension with a tall, thinly proportioned tower or bell-cote and, in some cases, when combined with the low side walls, results in the appearance of more roof than wall.

Gothic Revival (1830-1900)

While many features, including coloured slate roofs, rock-faced stone walls with smooth stone trimming, may be similar to other contemporary styles, such as the Victorian Romanesque, the pointed arch in various profiles and sizes distinguishes the Victorian Gothic. (5–24, Brockville; 5–25, St. Mary's)

5–24

5–25

In spite of the Classical profile and symmetrical composition, the battlements and pointed arches distinguish these early Gothic Revival churches. (5–26, Jordan; 5–27, Cobourg)

5–26

5–27

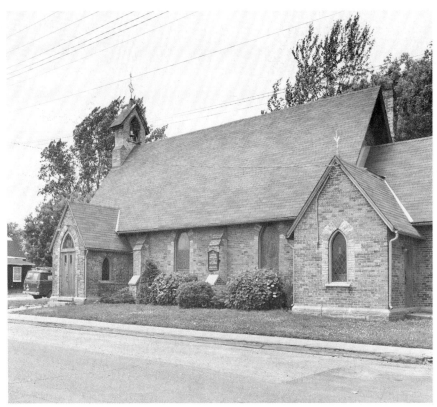

5—28

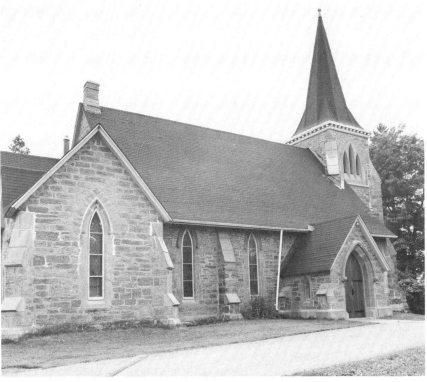

5—29

The thin bell tower or bell-cote, perched on the ridge of the broad roof, combined with low walls and side-porch entrances mark the smaller rural churches influenced by the Anglican Cambridge Camden Society. (5—28, Cardinal; 5—29, Hawkesbury)

5—30
A vernacular interpretation of the traditional bell-cote distinguishes this twentieth century entrance porch. (South Porcupine)

A steep roof pitch and Gothic arcading embellish the otherwise simple board-and-batten technique. (5—31, Gravenhurst; 5—32, Point Edward)

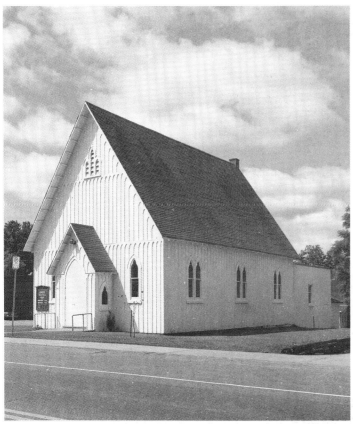

5—31

5—32

Chapter 6 Italian Villa (1830-1900)

Morrisburg

The Italian Villa style was a Classical alternative to the contemporary Gothic Revival style. The Italian Villa embraced the irregular outline and composition of the picturesque, but for the most part rejected the pointed windows, steep roofs and vergeboards of the Gothic in favour of Classical details. In a manner of speaking, the Italian Villa is the first Ontario style that clearly breaks from past colonial traditions by blending the variety of the picturesque with the balance and harmony of Classical architecture romantically inspired from northern Italian country houses or villas.

The most striking feature of this style is the tall tower or campanile with balconied window located at the corner or juncture of the L-shaped plan. In addition to this tower, other characteristics described by the English architect J. C. Loudon, in his *Encyclopaedia* of 1833, include irregular massing, closely spaced or grouped windows, at times arched, a portico, an arcade or loggia and a mildly pitched roof with cantilevered eaves. The chimneys in large villas are often grouped and decorated with a blind arcade and topped with a pronounced cornice. A. J. Downing, the American, quickly followed suit with several publications, among them *Cottage Residences*, 1840, and *Architecture of Country Houses*, 1850, providing variations on the theme that he loosely labelled Tuscan, Romanesque, Bracketted and even Rhinish. Acknowledging the common aspiration to achieve the picturesque, early examples of this style share similar materials and details with the Regency. However, by the third quarter of the nineteenth century the Italian Villa matured into an urban exercise in architectural sophistication. The simple composition of the Tuscanlike mode set in the rural environment, as seen in Bellevue, near Kingston (see 6–3), had developed by the late nineteenth century into complicated and enriched compositions. The Leadly House in Toronto (see 6–2) represents the Late Victorian version of the villa, with its large proportions, variety of textures and shapes and heavy embellishments. As Downing himself appropriately remarked, the Italian Villa style expressed not country life or town life, "...but a mingling of both." In other words, it was never rural Gothic or city Georgian, but a blend of the two.

6–1

The distinguishing features of the Italian Villa are evident in this drawing from Downing's Cottage Residences, *1840. Notable features include:*

- *campanile or tower, with entrance and hip roof*
- *balconied windows*
- *side loggia or veranda*
- *terrace*
- *grouped chimney*
- *bold but simple window surrounds*
- *bracketted eaves*

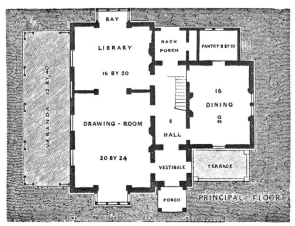

6–2

Exuberance in detailing compounded by variation in colour or texture as well as a change in proportion, such as tall tower and thin windows, are more typical of the later nineteenth century Victorian version of the villa. (Leadly House, 1876, Toronto, now home of the Felician Sisters) Notable features of this Victorian Italian Villa include:

- *elaborately decorated large veranda*
- *narrow windows with single one-over-one paned sash windows*
- *patterned and dichromatic brickwork*
- *paired console brackets with drops or pendants similar to the Italianate style*
- *oversized dentil blocks*
- *tent-shaped metal window hood reminiscent of earlier Regency examples*
- *accentuated keystones and impost blocks*
- *multishaped dormer*
- *steep roof with metal curbs*

6—3

One of the first Ontario Italian villas in the Tuscan mode, this house shares with the Regency style a preference for a stucco exterior finish, French doors and an exotic flair in such details as the awninglike hood over the balconied window, the vergeboards and the acutely tapered finial. (Bellevue, ca. 1838-40, Kingston, George Browne, architect)

6—4

In spite of its neglected condition and abandoned state this Italian villa maintains its distinguishing characteristics. The tall campanile with encircling balcony is particularly noteworthy as a Victorian embellishment of the more modest Tuscan campanile. (Bradford)

6–5
Unusual are symmetrical villas, such as this rambling brick example with central tower flanked by semioctagonal pavilions. (Guelph)

6–6

6–7

With minor adjustments for details and materials, these villas closely resemble Downing's published model. (6–6, Niagara-on-the-Lake; 6–7, Woodstock)

Italian Villa (1830-1900)

6—8
An exhibition of many styles, an eclectic array of academic details and mixture of forms become a prism of late-nineteenth century architectural styles. (Morrisburg)

6—9
*A strong Gothic accent is provided by this
board-and-batten villa with steep roofs,
gables and vergeboards. (VanKleek Hill)*

6—10
*The essence of the Italian villa is given a
minimal and vernacular expression in
these identical houses, in spite of the loss
of one tower's roof. (Cornwall)*

Chapter 7 Italianate (1850-1900)

Dundas

The Italianate is not a revival of a past architectural style, period or type. Rather than placing an emphasis on standard historical details or a recognizable composition such as the Italian Villa style, the Italianate prefers to stylize and exaggerate selected features, often repeating the motif several times across the building. This is most evident in commercial buildings, where mass production of cast-iron architectural elements provided great quantities of details easily applied around doors and windows and along cornices and parapets.

The Italianate house is generally distinguished from the Villa style by the lack of the prominent corner tower. High-style examples are characterized by a rooftop cupola or belvedere, ornately decorated cornice brackets and deep projecting eaves. Dichromatic effects created by contrasting materials and colours are found around windows and at corners. Exaggerated window cornices based on the stilted segmental arch are also very popular. For the most part details are Classical in origin, but being freely modified, detailing may take on Baroque exuberance, while at other times austere and highly stylized neo-Greek forms may be evident.

Since no particular architect championed the Italianate cause and no philosophy expounded its benefits, the origins of this style remain elusive. However, due to the great quantity of Italianate examples throughout North America, the fabricated and almost artificial quality of this style has been aptly described as "synthetic eclecticism." The Italianate stretches the confines of academic eclecticism by distorting the individual historical elements, then synthesizes them into a "new" arrangement devoid of that historicism normally associated with academic or analytical eclecticism. This manner of eclecticism found its greatest appeal in the United States, and to a lesser extent in Ontario. Italianate houses with their distinctive belvederes, oversized cornice brackets and repetitive cast-iron eyebrowlike window trim were built in urban as well as rural areas.

However, unique to Ontario, a vernacular version of the Italianate style befitting "synthetic eclecticism" was introduced when *The Canada Farmer* journal in 1865 presented to its readers a two-storey dwelling with projecting frontispiece covered with a mildly pitched hip roof that the editors described as "simply designed," with "no attempt to make it all corners and gables," adding, "It is simply a straightforward square house." Perhaps the editors felt that their clientele, tired of the Gothic Revival, would now prefer something more Classical in form. *The Canada Farmer* presented to the rural and farming population a house truly representative of mid-nineteenth century Victorian Ontario.

The house possesses the traditional Georgian balance and square shape, but when compared to eighteenth century examples, it is in fact richer in ornamentation and texture, including eyebrowlike window cornices, heavy roof-cornice brackets and contrasting coloured materials. To this model was often added an eclectic combination of some rural Gothic feature, such as vergeboards or lancet windows, a variety of Classical details and wall finishes, executed in the typically stylized or exaggerated mode of the American Italianate style. Characteristic of the Ontario psyche, *The Canada Farmer* house is an accomplished compromise. It satisfies the desire to be modern or up-to-date with Italianate features, but not lavishly so.

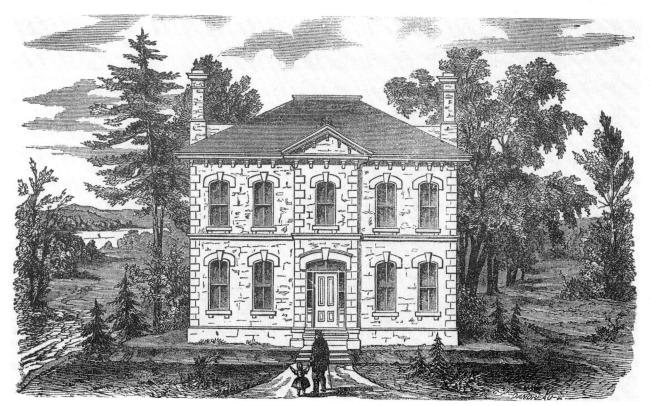

7−1

Noteworthy features on this model house from **The Canada Farmer** *include:*
– hip roof with deck
– pedimented projecting frontispiece
– strongly accentuated corners
– eyebrowlike segmentally arched window cornices
– large-paned sash-type windows
– tall chimneys

Italianate (1850-1900)

The model *Canada Farmer* house was successfully accepted with some modifications. Whether one or two stories tall and three or five bays across, the house is given a dichromatic (two-colour) effect by accentuating brick walls with stone dressings for quoins, window cornices, lintels and string courses. In later examples, patterned concrete blocks replaced the more expensive cut-stone details. The Brown-Vooro House, circa 1870, in Meadowvale (see 7–3) is an excellent example of a vernacular Italianate adaptation of *The Canada Farmer* house. The formal or Georgian symmetry and Classical details are highlighted by an acutely pointed Gothic-like gable trimmed with vergeboard. Large cornice brackets have a similar profile and spacing as those of *The Canada Farmer* house.

7–2

An excellent variation on **The Canada Farmer** *house is well-illustrated in this example. (Grimsby)*

7-3
Noteworthy features on this vernacular interpretation of The Canada Farmer
house include: (Brown-Vooro House, Meadowvale, Mississauga)
- *large cornice brackets*
- *formal balance of parts*
- *Gothic-like gable with vergeboards*
- *quoins*
- *hip roof with tall chimneys*
- *roof cresting in the form of Classical Greek antefixae*

7—4

Notwithstanding the varied finishes and details, vernacular interpretations of The Canada Farmer *prototype continued the Georgian traditions of formal and symmetrical compositions centred about a projecting frontispiece. (7—4, Belleville; 7—5, Ancaster; 7—6, London)*

7-5

7-6

Italianate (1850-1900)

7-7
High-style Italianate details are emphatically expressed with paired cornice brackets mirrored by scroll-like window corbels or consoles supporting elaborately carved window cornices. (London)

7-8
Projecting roof eaves with paired cornice brackets repeated on the bay window and veranda combined with a pedimented roofline and window cornices provide strong Italianate accents to an otherwise vernacular framed dwelling. (Thunder Bay)

7–9
Ideally the Italianate house with a cube or tall square proportion would be richly decorated and crowned with a rooftop belvedere or cupola. (Napanee)

Italianate (1850-1900)

Variations on the ideal square Italianate with cupola can be seen in the following examples. (7–10, Ancaster; 7–11, Newmarket; 7–12, Prescott)

7–10

7–11

7–12

7-13

7-14

7-15

The square Italianate could also be simply expressed in vernacular form (7-13, Pembroke) or embellished with historically correct Classical details (7-14, St. Catharines) or enriched with an eclectic blend of freely adapted features (7-15, London).

Italianate (1850-1900)

7–16
Typical high-style, mass-produced decorative cast-iron detailing is abundantly evident on this commercial block. The visual continuity ends abruptly in the last four bays, where the absence of those details results in a flat surface. This building, which combines commercial shops with apartments above, is of interest to those who believe that mixed-use is a novel twentieth century development. (Dundas)

7-17

7-18

7-19

7-20

The L-shaped plan popular in the Gothic Revival style was also variously adapted or finished with Italianate features, including strong dichromatic brick accents (7-17, Troy), an eclectic mix of stone trimming and a projecting cornice with paired brackets (7-18, St. Catharines), repetitive cornice brackets and window cornices (7-19, Belle River) and in some cases the L-shaped plan and details are minimally expressed (7-20, Cobourg). The Cobourg house also retains the removable winter or storm porch, once a common feature on many Ontario houses.

Italianate (1850-1900)

7-21
A traditional Italianate façade with paired cornice brackets and eyebrowlike window cornices shares a streetscape with a dichromatic enriched Victorian Gothic façade, identified by the acutely pointed arched windows and exaggerated cornice elements. (Prescott)

7-22
In spite of the loss of the probably cast-iron or sheet-metal roof cornice, the remaining double-tiered brick corbelling, dichromatic quoins and repetitive cast-iron window cornices identify the Italianate features of this commercial block. (Smiths Falls)

Chapter 8 Octagon (1850-1880)

Brampton

While Orson Fowler is more widely known for his expertise in phrenology, the popular pseudoscience of analyzing personality traits from the bumps and shape of the head, in 1849 he published *A Home for All*, which provided him a place in the history of North American architecture. In order to satisfy two basic phrenological needs, "inhabitiveness and constructiveness," Fowler advocated that everyone should not only build his own home but that it should have eight sides.

The inspiration for the octagon shape was predicated not so much on aesthetic merit but simply that a polygon with eight sides was the most practical linear shape to construct that approximated the circle or sphere, the form Fowler believed to be nature's ideal. In very practical terms, Fowler showed mathematically how the octagon contains one-fifth more room than a comparably sized square. An ardent believer in nature, economy and utility, Fowler preferred simplicity in details to an overabundance of either Gothic or Classical decorative elements. He promoted the innovative use of the gravel or concrete wall, which he thought to be naturally in great abundance and inexpensive, and easily constructed without the high costs of professional or skilled labour. Fowler reinforced his belief with practical experience, relaying to his readers how he had built for himself a large three-storey, eight-sided "gravel wall" house in upstate New York—which unfortunately was demolished in the late nineteenth century (see 8—1). In addition to the unique eight-sided shape and concrete building material, some other characteristic and innovative features of Fowler's New York Octagon include: four tiers of encircling verandas; a rooftop belvedere or lookout; gravel walls rusticated or scored to imitate cut stone; fresh-air ventilators and speaking tubes to all levels; hot and cold water; indoor water closet; and gas heat and illumination. In addition to Fowler's personal residence, *A Home for All* illustrated plans and elevations for a variety of different types of eight-sided buildings, including churches, schools and barns.

Octagon (1850-1880)

Throughout his life, Fowler travelled and lectured extensively, including in Ontario. *A Home for All* had two major editions and nine printings. Fowler's writings on phrenology were published in several languages and by the 1860s the popularity of Octagons had spread throughout Canada and the United States. In practice, the economical and practical benefit of eight-sided houses and the "gravel wall" became accepted, but not everyone shared Orson Fowler's utilitarian architectural concepts or agreed with phrenology, and Octagons often exhibited a variety of stylistic influences, from Georgian to Second Empire, reflective of the traditional styles of the period.

8–1

Fowler's own imposing Octagon is noted for simplicity in detail highlighted with encircling verandas and a rooftop lookout or belvedere providing the occupants with a choice of vistas, whether in sun or shade at any time of the day.
Imparting a romantic allure to the property are the historically derivative Gothic Revival ogee arches with ball finial topping each belvedere window and the arcaded roof trim above. Features derived from practical consideration include the plain squared veranda posts and brackets, simple balustrades and a raised first storey that allowed ample light into the basement level, where kitchen, laundry and other support services were located. More in keeping with traditional Classical styles are the shuttered multipaned sash windows, main entrance framed by straight transom and sidelights; unusual are the paired doors on the upper floor verandas. As Fowler recommended, the "gravel walls" were probably covered with stucco and scored to imitate cut stone. (Illustration is from Fowler's A Home for All*)*

8-2
Stuccoed walls scored to imitate cut stone or ashlar and paired windows follow Fowler's advice, but personal aesthetics deviated from the ideal Octagon. The mansard roof, bracketted and moulded cornice, round-arched dormer windows covered by gabled roofs and fanciful veranda brackets are evidence of Second Empire stylistic influences. (Hawkesbury)

8-3
This recently restored Octagon was constructed following a number of Fowler's suggestions, including the "gravel wall" technique, encircling verandas, rooftop lookout and an absence of add-on decorative enrichments with obvious stylistic influences. (Bracebridge)

Octagon (1850-1880)

8—4
This gabled Octagon has red brick façades accentuated in vernacular fashion with white stone for quoins, keystones and impost blocks. The thin window apertures filled with large-paned sashes are indicative of a relatively late nineteenth century date of construction. (Cobden)

8—5
The absence of any rooftop lookout, belvedere or cupola is not uncommon on smaller or modest Octagons. In such examples it is usual to find the chimney placed along one end wall, as in this example. The corner pilasters with moulded bases and capitals provide strong Classical accents to the rough-cast stuccoed walls. The enclosed entrance porch and fenestration appear to have been altered during the mid-twentieth century. (Brampton)

8–6
This brick Octagon with low monitorlike belvedere is highlighted with traditional stylistic elements. Of particular note are the Neoclassical features, including the thin pilasters accentuating each forty-five-degree angle, the fanlight transom over the entrance and the denticulated belvedere cornice. The paired cantilever brackets of the main cornice are popular Regency-style features. The two-tiered portico appears to be of early twentieth century vintage. (Maple)

8–7
This plain stuccoed Octagon, distinguished by a squared belvedere and large paired chimneys, is adapted from a plan for a small Octagon outlined in A Home for All. *(Bowmanville)*

8–8
A hip-roof variant of the Octagon with stucco walls and central chimney.
(Picton)

8–9
A low one-storey brick version with tall French doors opening onto a veranda
crowned by a clerestory monitor. (Brampton)

Chapter 9 Romanesque Revival (1850-1900)

Woodstock

Like the Gothic Revival, this style had its origins in nineteenth century romanticism. But rather than drawing on the pointed architecture of the Gothic, the round-arched examples of the earlier Romanesque were chosen. In Europe the Romanesque began in the ninth century when Charlemagne, emperor of the Holy Roman Empire, revived an interest in the arched forms of the earlier Roman Empire. His architectural lead found acceptance and was developed with regional modifications throughout western Europe during the next two centuries, and culminated in the great cathedrals, abbeys and monastic churches of France in the twelfth century. As a result of its broad geographical distribution, stylistic variations became known by region or ruling authority–i.e., Lombardian for northern Italy, Carolingian for Emperor Charlemagne, Norman for England, and so on.

Belonging to an earlier historical period, the round-arched Romanesque was at first considered primitive: the nineteenth century mind interpreted it as merely a prelude to the more sophisticated Gothic style. Thus this style was not as widely accepted as the more advanced Gothic Revival style. However, the monumental scale, decorative richness, bold and at times lavish use of materials characteristic of the mature Romanesque Revival became very suitable for civic building and symbolic of the urban affluence following Confederation in 1867. Romanesque Revival is at times so similar to Gothic Revival that the existence of either rounded or pointed windows is perhaps the chief distinction between the two revival styles.

The popularity of Romanesque Revival in the last decades of the nineteenth century was in large part due to the genius of the American architect H. H. Richardson, whose examples were so instrumental and widely emulated that this style often carries his name. Fresh from academic training at the Ecole des Beaux-Arts in Paris, he relied heavily on historical precedents, particularly those from southern France and northern Spain. He quickly left the archaeological copying to develop a very personal architectural expression centred more on architectural space and forms

77

Romanesque Revival (1850-1900)

9-1
*University College, University of Toronto,
1856, Cumberland and Storm. Notable
features of this Romanesque Revival
include:*
- *reliance on the rounded arch for
  openings and windows*
- *compound arched entry enriched with
  a variety of medieval mouldings*
- *arcaded cornice and string courses*
- *square tower with corner buttresses
  and decorative battlements*
- *roof cresting*

than on historical detail. His mature designs excelled in the straight-forward bold composition of complex masses or forms while integrating simplified and stylized decorative elements covered with unifying broad roof shapes. Characteristic features of his designs include a rock-faced stone finish, sparse distribution of openings, square-headed transomed windows arranged in rows of three or four, highly selective decorative motifs and the very typical and much copied wide-arched entry.

One of the earliest examples of the Romanesque Revival in Ontario, predating Richardson's work, is University College at the University of Toronto (see 9–1). Designed in 1856 by Cumberland and Storm, it exemplifies English Norman architecture with its round-headed windows, towers and stone walls accentuated with historically derivative mouldings, enrichments and a compound semicircular arched entry. While formal and nearly symmetrical in general appearance, a concession to the romantic's picturesqueness is made through the broken roofline enhanced by the offset corner turret on the central tower and by the decorative iron cresting along the peaks and ridges of the various hipped and gabled roofs. In the United States, a similar development occurred when, in 1846, James Renwick designed the first museum building for the Smithsonian Institute in the Romanesque Revival style. In a manner of speaking, both buildings were a springboard for their own country's academic version of the Romanesque Revival. Richardson's efforts in the 1870s were largely responsible for a more typically Victorian interpretation of the Romanesque that allowed more variety in form, inventiveness in composition and considerable exaggeration in detail.

9—2
Oxford County Courthouse, Woodstock, 1892, Cuthbertson and Fowler. Notable features of this Victorian Romanesque include:

- *extensive use of round arch*
- *heavy stone string courses*
- *dichromatic stonework accentuating openings, string courses*
- *heavy transom bars dividing windows*
- *arched entry supported by short polished columns*
- *round corner buttresses and oversized finials*
- *giant oriel window*

9—3
Oversized handrail newel post (Oxford County Courthouse, Woodstock)

9—4
Side entrance detail. (Oxford County Courthouse, Woodstock)

In Ontario, by the 1890s this round-arched revival in the Richardsonian or Victorian version had gained considerable popularity for civic and commercial architecture, including city halls and office buildings. The more academic version, archaeologically inspired and emulating historical precedents, remained favoured for church buildings. On the domestic side, private residences were massive in scale and their overall shape is reminiscent of the contemporary Queen Anne style, with multishaped roofs and eclectic mixing of details not only from medieval but at times Classical sources.

An excellent example of the Victorian or post-Richardson Romanesque is the Oxford County Courthouse, 1892, by Cuthbertson and Fowler. Retaining Norman building traditions with its squared tower, heavy stone walls and extensive use of round arches (see 9—4), this courthouse also presents a somewhat picturesque image with its irregular roofline and asymmetrical composition (see 9—2). Regardless of the intentions, the manner in which the details and forms were treated and the scale of the elements result in a unique building. No longer confined to historical prototypes, the Late Victorian architect exaggerated features and distorted proportions, creating a monumental, imposing and formidable composition. Distortion becomes apparent in such details as the "newel post" and the "handrail," which are of little practical benefit

Romanesque Revival (1850-1900)

to the user. And if a real hand were large enough to grasp the handrail, the body certainly could not pass through the arch (see 9–3). A structural ambiguity is also suggested where the oversized keystone in the second-floor window is proportionately taller and much more massive than the undersized columns that support the larger and heavier arched entry. Other exaggerations of details can be seen in the corner buttresses, which appear more like turrets than corner reinforcement, and in the oversized finials lining the gables and tower. Ambiguity of function is likewise seen in the two-storey projecting oriel window. Supported by a single but massive combination column-pedestal, the oriel's three tall arched windows light the upper-floor chamber. But what interior level is lighted by the small rectangular windows is not evident from the exterior elevation. Such ambiguities and distortions, from a purist's viewpoint, may seem deplorable as untruths, yet they exhibit the skilful and free manipulation of architectural forms and details so representative of the eclectic imaginations of the late nineteenth century Victorian mind.

The Romanesque Revival was not restricted to English Norman examples. Cathedrals from the Normandy region of France, with their twin-towered façade, also provided models for emulation,

9–5
St. Patrick's, Toronto. Notable features of this French Romanesque Revival include:
- *round arched openings of various sizes, usually thin with a vertical emphasis*
- *twin towers of approximately the same size*
- *corner buttresses of slight projection*
- *sparse use of string courses and mouldings*
- *three-arched portal*
- *a gallery or arcade of windows*
- *tall triple-arched windows lighting the nave*
- *arched niche for statuary*

particularly in Quebec, but also in French-speaking areas of Ontario. St. Patrick's in Toronto, employing the round arch to span openings, clearly sets itself apart from contemporary churches in the Gothic Revival style. With its monochromatic stone finish, buttresses of mild projection and orderly vertical emphasis expressed through its twin towers, St. Patrick's is distinct from the overstated detailing, irregular forms and complicated configuration of the Victorian Romanesque.

9-6
A vernacular variant of the Richardsonian Romanesque. (Sault Ste. Marie)

9-7
Representative of the Richardsonian version of the Romanesque Revival is this rock-faced stone office building with generous arched openings combined with narrow transomed windows arranged in groups of two, three or four. Also typical is the symmetrical composition, lack of historical enrichments and the short columns of the arched entry. (Sault Ste. Marie)

Romanesque Revival (1850-1900)

9-8
The essential features of this eclectic Romanesque Revival are outlined in stone. Rock-faced stone trimmings are used for massive lintels, round arches and string courses, and a symmetrical composition imparts an almost Classical appearance. Medieval elements include brick chequerboard patterns and a parapet gable topped with finials. Transomed windows are imaginatively formed by enlarging the uppermost cross bar of each window. The steep hip roof is similar to the Château style. (Caledonia)

Other variations freely adapted to public buildings. (9-9, St. Marys; 9-10, St. George)

9-9

9-10

9–11
A variation on the Romanesque corner-tower church plan. (Arnprior)

Romanesque Revival (1850-1900)

9–12
Round-arched apertures used for nave, clerestory and tower. (North Bay)

9–13
A variety of Romanesque fenestration applied to a residence with a multisloped roof and tower. (Hamilton)

9–14
The Beaux-Arts Classical entrance of this church creates an eclectic variation on the French Romanesque style. (Hawkesbury)

9–15
Multicoloured and patterned slate roofs are popular not only on Victorian Romanesque buildings but other late-nineteenth century styles. (Gananoque)

Romanesque Revival (1850-1900)

9–16
The essence of the Romanesque Revival, semicircular arches set against a smooth brick wall divided by thin pilaster strips and plain brick corbelling, is succinctly captured in this industrial building. (Sudbury)

9–17
While the plan and form of this church is not unique to the Romanesque Revival, the reliance on the round arch distinguishes it from the Gothic Revival. Semicircular hood-moulds, shared with the Italianate style, outline openings, and the arcaded corbel table trims the roof and tower cornices. (Windsor)

9–18
Completely executed in red brick, this church possesses typical Romanesque Revival elements. These include a tall tower with battered or tapered sides pierced with a variety of narrow arched openings; an arcaded portico or narthex and a series of arched nave windows above; stepped corbel table and archivolt trimming. However, the brickwork, windows and roof shape of the round tower relate more to the Château style. (Windsor, St. Andrew's Presbyterian)

Chapter 10   Second Empire (1860-1900)

Mallorytown

The name "Second Empire" is derived from the official style popular in France and its colonies during the reign of Napoleon III (1852-1870). Sometimes this style is erroneously called "Third Empire" after Louis Napoleon III, referring to his lineage—his uncle was Napoleon I—rather than Second Empire—the period he ruled as emperor. Inspired by such French examples as the ornate Paris Opéra and the 1850s additions to the Louvre, this style was transplanted to the United States and Canada, where it experienced short-lived popularity for large public and civic buildings. On non-governmental buildings, private dwellings and small commercial structures, the massive size, lavishness and grandeur of the French prototypes were subdued; yet the essence of the French examples, where not academically interpreted, was at least emulated from secondary sources, such as pattern books and trade journals.

Many of the finest examples of the style in Ontario have unfortunately been demolished, including the General Post Office on Adelaide Street in Toronto (see 10—1). The post office was remarkable for its complexity of forms and Classical enrichments on a relatively grand scale that could easily have competed with the best European examples. The main elevation, highlighted with a three-tiered pedimented frontispiece, was crowned by a bulbous mansard roof and a large clock with an enriched cornicelike hood. Straight-sided mansard roofs topped each corner pavilion in a towerlike manner and the roof slopes were punctuated by pedimented dormers with moulded surrounds. Detailed iron crest work provided a delicate finish to the otherwise overpowering composition. The grandness of the building was heightened by raising the ground-floor paired columns on a tall pedestal to include a squared plinth and a dado enriched with carved panels.

In vernacular tradition, often the most recognizable stylistic feature is the mansard roof (see 10—12). The profile of the roof may be straight, convex, concave or a combination of the three, covered with multicoloured slates and punctuated by dormers of various shapes and sizes (see 10—15). The formal appearance of

Second Empire (1860-1900)

the overall composition may be heightened by a projecting central frontispiece that at times continues upward, forming a distinct tower; when the projection occurs at the ends or corners of a building, as in the Toronto post office, this feature may be referred to as a pavilion. When the tower is placed off-centre, the asymmetrical balance of the façade creates a picturesque quality not unlike that found in late examples of the Italian Villa style. Typical of late nineteenth century building practices, windows are large, with only one or two panes or lights per sash, and may be round, segmental or at times pointed; they are most often framed with enriched surrounds and mouldings. The cornice is often embellished in fashion similar to the Italianate, with brackets, large blocks and a decorated frieze. Though stone is preferred, brick is often used, but regardless of the material, the exterior is invariably enriched with Classical mouldings and detail around door and window apertures, as well as corners, where heavy rustication or

10−1
The 1880s archival photograph of the General Post Office in Toronto (constructed 1869-73; demolished 1958) demonstrates the complexity of forms, richness of detail, as well as the scale of the formal and official version of the Second Empire style, as interpreted by trained academic architect Henry Langley. The person to the right of the entrance, leaning on the column's pedestal, provides a gauge of the building's size. (Photograph from the Metropolitan Toronto Library, T12069)

quoins are employed. The entrance is often a double door, with glazed upper panels having coloured or etched glass. Large sweeping porches or wraparound verandas characteristic of the Queen Anne style are not popular in the formal symmetrical examples, but may be seen on the informal, asymmetrically balanced towered versions.

An Ontario academic example of the formal towerless version of the style is well-represented by this limestone house in Kingston (see 10–2). A mansard roof with a concave profile covered with coloured slates crowns a symmetrical façade enriched with numerous Classical elements. Rusticated pilasters and scroll-like consoles or brackets support the arched pediment of the frontispiece, while the double-door entry is defined by a moulded surround with keystone. Two generous bay windows with wide stone mouldings and cornices are each topped with iron crest work, as is the mansard roof. The cresting is also repeated along the side porches or piazzas. Smooth pilasters, heavy mouldings and carved keystones are other classically derived elements adapted to the lavish scale of the Second Empire style. While structurally unnecessary, the horizontally grooved monumental corner pilasters visually support the bracketted cornice with decorated frieze. Shorter versions of these rusticated pilasters also frame the entrance and the bay window.

10–2
This balanced façade of Classical details crowned by a mansard roof complete with iron cresting is an excellent example of the formal but towerless version of the Second Empire style that most often served as a town or city dwelling. (Kingston)

Second Empire (1860-1900)

The distinguishing feature of this vernacular interpretation of the Second Empire style near Amherstburg is the straight-sided mansard roof punctuated with three gable dormers (see 10–3). The mildly projecting frontispiece or entrance bay rises upward three stories, but, failing to continue beyond the roof ridge, never really becomes a true tower or pavilion. The symmetry of the façade is slightly disturbed by the octagonal bay to one side. Adding to the vernacular design of the house are the varied shapes for the window treatments, gabled dormers framing round-headed openings and the peaked second-floor window cornices. The rustication of the wood siding to imitate cut stone or ashlar is an attempt to emulate the grand high-style prototypes, such as the Kingston example. Common with many other examples are the cornicelike moulded roof curbs differentiating changes in roof pitch.

10–3
Vernacular expressions are seen in this formal-appearing house with peaked window cornices, gablelike dormers and imitation ashlar wood siding. (Amherstburg)

Variations on the formal or symmetrically balanced versions of the Second Empire style are seen in these examples from:
10−4 Hamilton   10−5 Petrolia
10−6 Brockville

10−4

10−5

10−6

Second Empire (1860-1900)

10-7

10-8

10-9

10-10

In comparison are these towered examples, whose silhouette or profile creates a picturesque effect similar to the Italian Villa style:

10-7 St. Marys	*10-9 Belleville*
10-8 Simcoe	*10-10 Morrisburg*

10—11
In spite of alterations and loss of some original detail, this tall brick house is of interest for its centre placement of a picturesque tower between pavilionlike projecting bays to either side.
(Mallorytown)

10—12
Formal Second Empire stylistic aspirations are given a vernacular expression in this cottagelike house highlighted by a scaled-down frontispiece entrance, bracketted cornice with decorated frieze and bell-cast mansard roof. (Jarvis)

93

Second Empire (1860-1900)

10–13
Devoid of many of its original embellishments, this commercial block still retains its distinctive mansard roof and projecting roof tower, as well as its coloured and patterned slate roof tiles. (Dundas)

10–14
A rare example of a residential row or terrace constructed as a single block in a formal interpretation of the Second Empire style is complete with central and end pavilions, with straight and curved mansard roofs punctuated by a variety of dormers. (Peterborough)

10—15
This unusual compound or double-slope mansard roof is divided horizontally by a pronounced intermediate cornice and vertically by metal flashing known as roof curbs. The entire roof is trimmed with decorative cresting. (Morrisburg)

Chapter 11

Renaissance Revival (1870-1910)

Toronto

The Renaissance Revival style was built in either one or two distinctive versions. One is the astylar, meaning a building without columns or pilasters, and the other is the columnar or with columns, including arches. The astylar design, derived from the Roman and Florentine prototypes, is simpler and plainer, while the columnar version, with origins in Venetian examples, is more elaborate in composition and richer in colouration. Both versions are formal in balance and harmony, reflecting a studied and academic interest in sixteenth century urban Italian palaces and town houses, not the Palladian country villas popularized by Lord Burlington in eighteenth century England. As a result of an urban setting and an official appearance, the Renaissance Revival was more successfully adapted to commercial buildings, banks and offices than to houses. In spite of the predominately secular nature of the Renaissance and a strong Ontario preference for the Gothic Revival, a few churches were built following Italian Renaissance examples.

In England as early as 1829, Charles Barry set the pace, in contrast to the then contemporary preference for the Greek Revival style, when he opted for an astylar Renaissance design for the Travellers' Club in London. In Ontario, a similar pattern, much inspired by Roman palazzi, was used by Kivas Tully when he designed the Bank of Montreal, Toronto, in 1845, which was demolished in the 1880s.

The columnless astylar design shares many common features with the private dwellings of sixteenth century Rome and Florence. Usually not more than three stories in height, each level is clearly defined with moulded string courses, and the top of the building is neatly terminated by a heavy cornice supported by large brackets. Typically, window surrounds with wide architrave trim have pronounced moulded sills and scroll-like brackets supporting cornices of alternating segmented and pedimented shapes. A sparse selection of building materials is employed: e.g., usually the more substantial rusticated ashlar on the ground floor, followed by a lighter-appearing polished stone or brick on the upper floors. The second floor, which in traditional Italian practice is the main floor or *piano nobile*, may be treated with more architectural embellishments. Since a tall roof is undesirable, a balustrade or parapet is often used to shield its slope, and if visible may be covered with red, tiles recalling the building's Italian origins.

In the columnar version, the façade is more elaborate, with a variety of columns, pilasters and arches, and much richer in textural treatment. Each level is strongly defined with a different Classical order. The heavier and more solid Doric or Ionic is preferred on the ground floor and the lighter but more ornate Corinthian, Composite or variations are employed on the upper floors. Rather than a string course dividing each level, a full entablature is often used; thus each floor articulated with its own order may include a decorated frieze and a projecting cornice, albeit smaller than the main roof cornice. Architectural members may be superimposed on top of one another, resulting in considerable depth and complexity. Building materials in the columned version are generally lavish, with low relief sculpture and a variety of finishes, including polished marble.

11-1
This view of Toronto Street, Toronto, illustrates the two versions of the Renaissance Revival style in Ontario. The one to the left is astylar, that is, without columns, and the one to the right with polished columns, arches and pilasters represents the more lavish columnar type. While these two contrast in finishes, apertures and enrichments, they share detail, scale and composition derived from Italian Renaissance models. The one on the left reflects early sixteenth century palazzi from Rome or Florence, and the one on the right, later sixteenth century Venetian examples. Deviating from the accepted rules of formal symmetry, the later addition of three bays to the extreme right, while executed in the same style, does create an unbalanced façade that is made all the more disturbing by the bleak gap on the opposing side, partially filled with a bland Post-Modern entrance. (Toronto)

11-2
Ontario churches were also inspired by sixteenth century Italian models, as evidenced by this design. (Toronto)

11-3
With the cornice and street-level shopfronts restored, this building would be very much similar to the astylar example in illustration 11-1. (Toronto)

11-4
Arched windows or openings highlight the main floor of this otherwise astylar composition, whose façade is uniquely marked by multipaned metal casement windows. (Toronto)

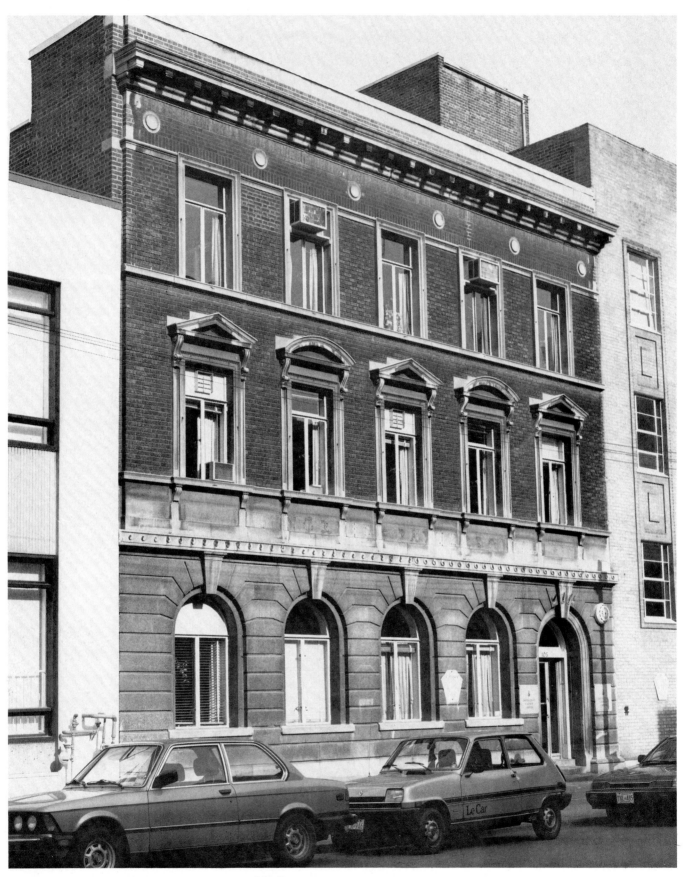

11—5
Academically interpreted Renaissance architectural elements enhance this office building. (Toronto)

11−6
Characteristic of Late Victorian aesthetics, these Renaissance features are
exaggerated and accentuated by dichromatic brickwork. (Ottawa)

Chapter 12

Queen Anne (1880-1910)

Brampton

The Queen Anne style is a panoply of decorative elements and varied forms manipulated into an imaginative and at times witty visual display. This style has less to do with Queen Anne (1702-14) than with the "Shavian Manorial style" developed during the second half of the nineteenth century by the English architect Richard Shaw. Shaw's unique adaptation of the Medieval asymmetrical and rambling Elizabethan country house, combined with Classical elements of the English Renaissance derived from houses of the early eighteenth century, including the reign of Queen Anne, became an inspiration to many architects on both sides of the Atlantic. Shaw crafted a unified composition of half-timbering, tiled and brick walls with steep cathedral-like roof shapes and tall chimneys. The highly decorated surfaces, enhanced with a selective application of Classical features, were punctuated by an assortment of randomly spaced windows. It is a mixture of elements from these two origins, Medievalism and early eighteenth century Classicism, that architects, particularly on this side of the Atlantic, interpreted and reorganized with considerable liberty and imagination into what today we know as the Queen Anne style.

Typical of the North American Queen Anne style is the irregular outline or silhouette, consisting of towers, broad gables or pediments, projecting two-storey bays, multisloped roofs and tall decorated chimneys. These forms are covered with a variety of materials of different textures and shapes. As many as three kinds of siding may be used on the same house: brick on the first floor, horizontal boards on the second and wood or terra-cotta tiles on the gables. Furthermore, the profiles and slopes of the materials may change from gable to gable: e.g., hexagonal shingles on one and fish scale on the other. Floriated and geometric motifs in terra cotta or stone decorate panels, belt courses, gables and window heads or lintels. Classically derived elements, such as the Palladian window, swan's neck pediment and mouldings of garlands or swags may highlight selected areas, and at other times Gothic or Medieval forms appear. Several open covered areas including verandas, balconies and porches under gables or eaves may be found on one house. Wood supporting members may be large and appear oversized, while trim is often intricate, complex and even delicate in comparison. Roofs have almost as many shapes as they do slopes: e.g., gable, hip and conical may cover one house. Tall multiple chimneys are often top-heavy, their sides embellished with terra-cotta panels or patterned brickwork. Iron cresting, finials and railings highlight the ridges and peaks of the roofs. Windows vary in size and shape, and the glazing of the sash consists of very large single or double panes, often with a transom above of coloured glass. Round or oval windows may accentuate a tower, stair hall, or even a chimney. Window heads, either straight or arched, may be executed in a different material from the walls and may be treated with carvings or other decorative motifs.

An excellent academic example of the style in Ontario is the house designed by Power & Son, architects, which was given a full-page illustration in the March 1888 issue of the *Canadian Architect and Builder* (see 12–1). The house is noteworthy for its retention of original features, including the multicoloured slate roof, normally one of the first elements to fall victim to modern repairs and renovations. A profusion of decorative motifs in stone,

12–1
An asymmetrical composition with towers of varying height, tall chimneys, decorative work and keyhole arched-entrance veranda highlight this example. (Kingston)

12-2
Keyhole profiled front porch of house illustrated in 12-1.

brick and wood is combined with a variety of roof shapes to create the richly decorated irregular form so characteristic of this style. Among the more prominent features are the central three-storey tower with tall hip roof, flanked by a large two-storey, three-sided bay with an open under-the-gable porch on one side and a two-storey corner tower with conical roof on the other side. The house also exhibits the original gabled entrance porch with sweeping veranda and decorative trim. Also very characteristic is the arch whose circumference approaches a closed circle, rather than a half-circle or less, as is most often the case. In profile this arch resembles a horseshoe—as in the porch of this house—or at times may be exaggerated when the sides and base are extended downward, forming a stylized keyhole (see 12-2).

In more modest and even vernacular terms, the essence of the Queen Anne style is succinctly expressed with wood in this timber-frame house in Keewatin (see 12-3). While simpler in composition and silhouette than the brick Kingston home, this example has no less than five different exterior treatments. Along the ground floor is a short skirting of vertical board-and-batten siding; then horizontal boards define the first floor and fish-scale wood shingles the second. Additionally, diagonal board-and-batten siding finish the gables, and a different shape of wood shingle is used to cover the roof slopes. Another characteristic often seen on buildings of timber and mixed construction is the flared second storey. Where the horizontal siding meets the different finish or material —in this case, wood shingles—there is a slight projection or flare to

12-3
Timber-frame house in vernacular Queen Anne style (Mathers-Walls House, Keewatin)

the upper surface. Other features derived from medieval sources include exaggerated roof curbs in the form of crenellations, the arcading of the roof deck railing and the Tudor or depressed arches of the veranda railing. The oversized corner consoles˙and vertical brackets supporting the spindle frieze are more typical of the intricate and complex veranda detailing of this style.

12—4
The exterior finish of this house is reminiscent of the popular American Stick style, but the massing of the composition and details, including the decorated chimney pierced by a window, are very characteristic of the mature Queen Anne style. (Brockville)

Queen Anne (1880-1910)

12—5
Much emulated throughout the province is the Queen Anne style at its most exuberant, as in this example. Of note is the oversized corner turret supported by one thin column and the two-tiered porch with elaborate wood turned posts and supporting trim. Adding variety is the large corner tower with conical cap and roof pierced by an attenuated through-the-cornice or wall dormer. (Sarnia)

12—6
More akin to the academic English Shavian Manorial style is this large brick house noted for asymmetrical massing, a broad hip roof and cross gables united by a centrally located octagonal tower whose one side is transformed into a massive chimney with multiple stacks. The casement windows with mullions and transoms are in keeping with the emulated Medieval building traditions. (Gananoque)

Other examples incorporating the tower or turret are variously expressed in the following:

12−7
Of note is the encircling veranda reflecting the shape of the tower. (Napanee)

12−8
The flared eaves of the tower are particularly evident. Also of interest is the gable, which is treated with a very large half-round, three-part window, framed by vergeboards, rather than the under-the-gable porch. (Thunder Bay)

Queen Anne (1880-1910)

12–9
This brick tower is appropriately corbelled at roof level. (London)

12–10
A variety of finishes distinguishes this example. Noteworthy is the upper-floor window configuration, where the upper sash is banded by small rectangular lights or panes. (Brampton)

Vernacular expressions of this style are individually composed in the following examples:

12−11
Variety of forms and massing are implied with the octagonal tower, cross gable and two-tiered porch and balcony. (Iroquois Falls)

12−12
The mature textbook example is scaled down, but the basics, including the variety of forms, asymmetrical massing and mixture of materials, are well-executed in brick, stone and shingle. (Thunder Bay)

Variations without the corner tower also exist:

12—13
An eclectic mixture of forms and details is strikingly evident in this composition, where a Palladian window inspired by Georgian Colonial architecture highlights the main gable and a keyhole arch embraces the entrance. (Bowmanville)

12-14
Brick, shingles, half-timbering and oriel windows recall medieval precedents.
(Thunder Bay)

12-15
The shortened veranda draws attention to the patterned brickwork along the sides of the three-sided stair-hall bay and the chimney. The gables also retain their decorated surfaces. (Pembroke)

The Queen Anne is also adapted to cottages, as in the following examples:

12–16
A streetscape filled with medieval-inspired surface enrichments. (London)

12–17
Hip roof, a complex façade with two gables and a veranda are mixed with a "Colonial"-inspired doorway and paired pilasters framing the window. (Belleville)

12−18
Through-the-cornice dormers, one with a hip roof and the other with a chipped gable or jerkin-head, increase the vertical quality of this technically one-and-a-half-storey cottage. (Tottenham)

12−19
A contrasting pair, similar in conception but not in detail and finishes. (Sault Ste. Marie)

Queen Anne (1880-1910)

12-20
Unadorned surfaces and simple wood treatment as expressed in the grouping of short veranda columns, cantilevered cornice brackets and plain brick walls are popular in the domestic version of Edwardian Classicism. (Sault Ste. Marie)

12-21
The uniform covering of shingles across gables and towers combined with a veranda highlighted in the Classical Ionic order are typical features associated with the Colonial Revival and American Shingle style. (St. Catharines)

12–22
Compare the early twentieth century wraparound corner veranda with squared pillars of this example to the turned posts, spindles and cutout brackets of the late nineteenth century porch to the right. The intricately carved and patterned gable is clearly of Queen Anne inspiration. (North Bay)

12–23
The complexity of built form and variety of decorative detailing is well illustrated in this unique balcony plus porch under gable. (Aurora)

Chapter 13 Château (1880-1940)

Ottawa

As the name indicates, the overall impression of this style, at least from a distance, gives the illusion of French sixteenth century châteaux from the Loire River region. It was during the reign of François I (1515-1547) that the Classicism of the Italian Renaissance was introduced into France and there combined with the existing Gothic traditions of the previous two centuries. In Canada, by the close of the nineteenth century this mixture or blend of stylistic influences resulted in a distinctive style that found favour among architects and their wealthy clients, including railway companies and governments from Halifax to Victoria.

In addition to the picturesqueness and grand informality, a most prominent characteristic of this style is a very high roof having a steep pitch often punctuated with many dormer windows. The silhouette of the metal-clad roof may be broken by towers, turrets, tourelles and finials. The scale, if not monumental, is large, rarely symmetrical, and the materials usually lavish. The favoured building material, cut stone, is either smooth or rock-faced. For reasons of economy, bricks are employed but trimmed with cut stone. The croisette or cross window combined with the depressed arch having a basket-handlelike profile is ideal because of the association with fifteenth century France. However, window and door apertures may be trimmed with Classical mouldings, while other areas have Gothic-inspired enrichments. Straight-headed sash windows with large single panes are popular on twentieth century examples. Oversized wall dormers decorated with both Gothic and Classical ornament are commonly found highlighting cornices and parapets along with smaller dormers higher up on the upper reaches of the roof slope.

During the first decades of the twentieth century, the Château style became a standard for railway stations, hotels and federal government buildings. With the completion of the transcontinental railway, Canadian Pacific sought an appropriate architectural expression for its new stations and hotels that would be recognizable as distinctly Canadian. H. Kalman, in his 1968 article "The Railway Hotels and the Development of the Château Style," examines the history of CP's hotels and stations, federal government buildings and other examples of this style as one of the first expressions of Canadian nationalism. CP's New York City architect, Bruce Price, designed many buildings, including the Hotel Frontenac in Quebec City (1892), establishing the Château style.

On the West Coast, this style was adopted by the English architect Francis Rattenbury for the design of the Empress Hotel in Victoria (1904). The Royal York Hotel in Toronto (1924-29), with its steep roof, smooth wall surface and select medieval detailing, is a late example of this style.

13-1
Formal in its balanced composition, arrangement of parts and disposition of detail, Chorley Park as seen in this archival photograph possesses distinct Château-style characteristics by combining medieval French Gothic features, including corner turrets or tourelles, steep roof, finials, cresting and croisette windows, with Classical embellishments around windows, dormers and chimney sides, as well as a very Classical design for an entrance and **porte-cochère** *or carriage porch. (Photograph of Government House, 1916, from Metropolitan Toronto Library, T11930)*

One of the finest academic interpretations of the Château style in Ontario was Chorley Park (1911), designed by F.R. Heaks, after plans by John Lyle, who earlier had studied in New York and France. While the façade was symmetrically balanced in the formal sense, the steep roofs have an abundance of corner turrets, or tourelles, chimney stacks, pedimented wall dormers, finials and crestings to create a picturesque effect. In form and detail, Chorley Park may have been the next best thing to actually having a French Renaissance château shipped from the Old World. The lavishness of its interior fittings and high maintenance costs were too easy an excuse for its unwarranted demolition in the 1950s.

Spurred by the desire for national identity, the federal government attempted to adapt Château characteristics to design guidelines for federal buildings. Under the auspices of the federal government the Château style was transformed, losing the picturesqueness and informality of the earlier examples. The new emerging forms were largely symbolic: stone construction reminiscent of vernacular French-Canadian buildings and tall roof shapes harmonious with the Parliament Buildings in the Gothic Revival style. This self-conscious attempt at a Canadian national style was most successful on small-scale buildings imbued with strong associations with the Canadian Colonial style. Larger landmark buildings, such as the Supreme Court Building, Ottawa, became marked by an unimaginative formal quality that was easily eclipsed after the Second World War by the very popular and mass-produced office buildings of the Late International style.

13-2
A definite Château-style quality is achieved with the steep metal-clad roof, battlemented tower, two tiers of small dormers and tall gabled wall dormers enriched with Gothic detailing reminiscent of French Renaissance prototypes. The corbelled projecting upper or attic floor mimics late Medieval fortified walls. (Château Laurier, Ottawa)

13-3

13-4

While not as grand in size or scale as Canada's Supreme Court building, these two buildings share a similar formalism in composition. (Ryerson Polytechnical Institute, Toronto, top and Supreme Court Building, Ottawa, below)

Château (1880-1940)

13–5
A Period Revival house with minimal Châteauesque elements most evident in the corner-tower entrance and large wall dormers with croisette window. (Toronto)

13–6
However picturesque from a distance, the solidity and security of the Medieval fortified château no doubt played a part in the design of this penitentiary. (Kingston)

13–7
Three tiers of hipped dormers highlight the roof slope. (Confederation Building, Ottawa)

13–8
Very typical of the mature Canadian Château style, this building includes rock-faced stone walls, croisette windows, tall wall dormers and steep metal-clad roofs with numerous dormers. (Confederation Building, Ottawa)

13—9
An octagonal "watch" tower marks this corner building with a distinctive Château-style roof with wall dormers. (Toronto)

Chapter 14 Beaux-Arts Classicism (1900-1945)

Owen Sound

Two fundamental factors led to establishing this Classical architectural style. One is the Ecole des Beaux-Arts in France, from which the style derives its name, and the other is the example set at the 1892 World's Columbian Exposition, held in Chicago.

During the last decades of the nineteenth century, a generation of architects had been disciplined in the formal Classical architectural language taught at the Ecole des Beaux-Arts in Paris. The programme required students to produce a variety of designs, including presentation drawings, elevations and plans, for large and complex buildings, based on formal rules of balance and symmetry, utilizing not only ancient Roman and Greek models but other Classical styles, including Italian and French Renaissance architecture. The strict academic training, the facility for architectural drawing and reliance on stylistic historicism resulted in buildings that, no matter how complex or simple in function, plan or elevation, always exhibited a clarity of form, albeit at times of magnificent proportions, defined with traditional Classical elements. The façade, often articulated with monumental columns or pilasters, always has a highly visible central entrance or frontispiece. Depending on the source of Classical inspiration, the building might be endowed with greater or lesser amounts of detailing and enrichments, i.e., plain unadorned surfaces typical of the Greek models, or the more ornamented late Roman and Renaissance styles.

The Chicago Exposition of 1893 provided a North American forum for selected architects to display Classical principles of design they had learned either directly at the Ecole des Beaux-Arts in Paris or secondhand from associates and publications. So prevalent was the undisguised and even pretentious templelike atmosphere that the exposition came to be known as the "White City of Roman Buildings." The exposition's obvious association with Classic architecture on a scale grander than that of ancient Rome was matched by an enthusiasm resulting in the construction of oversized Classical buildings throughout North America.

In Ontario, the American version of Beaux-Arts Classicism was not totally embraced. Ontario architects, with individual exceptions, preferred a Classical statement reflecting a more refined

123

interpretation of Roman and Greek architecture on a smaller scale rather than the heavy-handed American version. Additional influences in Ontario also came from direct exposure to French Classicism, such as the seventeenth century façades of the Louvre in Paris and early eighteenth century Classicism. The spatial interiors of fourth century Roman basilicas and baths also played a key role in the design of railway stations and banking halls, two types of buildings well-suited to Beaux-Arts Classicism. Regardless of the inspiration, the goal was to synthesize the Classical past by creating large and at times exuberant, if not grand, displays of templelike buildings adapted to a variety of public and semipublic uses, such as post offices, banks and libraries.

One may look upon Beaux-Arts Classicism as the ultimate expression, the apex or summit, of Classical eclecticism, begging the question, what could possibly be next? Attempts to develop a

14-1
The square building with entrance on the cutoff corner with templelike side façades was a pattern repeated in other banks. (Bank of Montreal, Toronto, 1885, Darling and Curry, architects)

"Modern Classicism" were marked by reducing the Classical elements to the bare essentials, whose details have an angular quality similar to the Art Deco style. However sincere such attempts to modernize the Classical vocabulary of antiquity, Beaux-Arts and Modern Classicism were criticized as being out of touch and not responsive to the "new aesthetic" of modernism formulated by the proponents of the International style.

The monumental scale of the Harbour Commission Building, Toronto (see 14–3), is reminiscent of the American version of Beaux-Arts Classicism. A screen of columns four stories in height is raised on a tall arcaded street or entrance level, which in turn is raised on a prominent foundation course. This compositional hierarchy, crowned by a strong cornice and an attic storey, forms what from a distance appears to be a colossal one-storey "temple," when upon close inspection the building possesses at least seven stories. Considering the building's once-upon-a-time physical proximity to the shore of Lake Ontario, one wonders if the client and architect had in mind that this twentieth century temple would be like a beacon guiding lake travelers to a safe harbour. Unlike mature American Beaux-Arts examples, this Ontario version prefers single columns with smooth shafts and unadorned mouldings and a plain cornice with modillion blocks rather than paired columns with enrichments, typical of American Beaux-Arts Classicism.

14–2
The form of the Toronto example minus the academic Beaux-Arts enrichments was repeated years later. (McMillan Block, Perth, 1903, Darling and Pearson, architects)

Beaux-Arts Classicism (1900-1945)

Reflecting Beaux-Arts architectural influences more directly from French sources and predating the American "Roman White City" is the Bank of Montreal, Toronto (see 14-1). Modest in size but rich in sculptural ornament, the composition, elements and details of this building have more in common with French Classicism than with the severe and monumental Roman architecture. However academic the detailing of this building is, in plan it adapts a common nineteenth century vernacular trait: the store with main entrance on the chamferred or cutoff corner. Very practical in that it provides an entrance visible to the intersecting streets, this corner plan was much copied by other commercial banks in both large and small centres throughout Ontario during the early twentieth century. Comparing this bank with the McMillan Block, Perth (see 14-2), reveals similarities of outline and forms as well as illustrates the development of Beaux-Arts Classicism from the academic to the vernacular.

14-3
The monumental columns and grand scale follow the American version of Beaux-Arts Classicism. (Harbour Commission Building, Toronto, 1917, Chapman and McGriffin, architects)

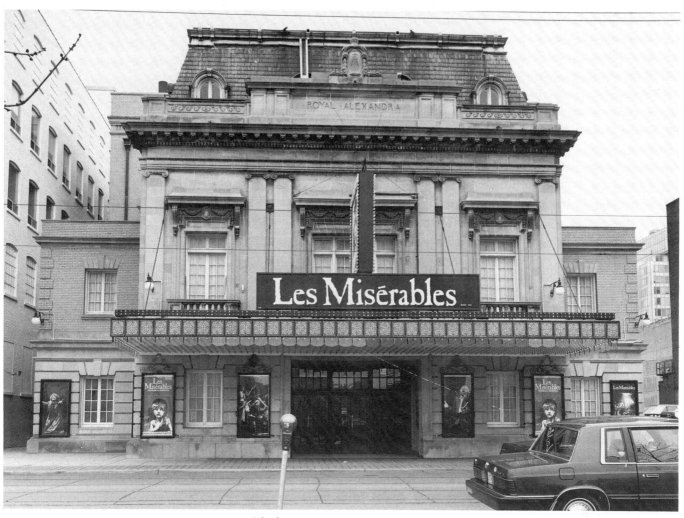

14—4

Though not monumental in size, behind the glass marquis is a fine but understated expression of Beaux-Arts Classicism of French inspiration. The façade, divided into three bays by pilasters with Ionic capitals, is symmetrically balanced by small recessed wings to each side and is crowned by a cartouche or crest with the initials of the theatre company. (The Royal Alexandra Theatre, Toronto, 1907, John M. Lyle, architect)

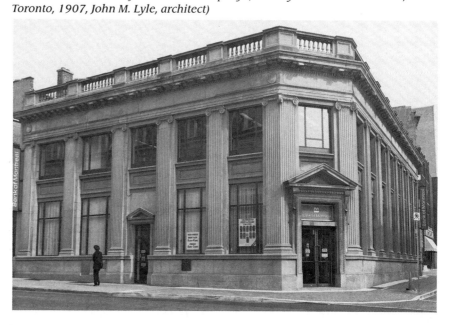

14—5
Clean and unadorned Classical elements. (London)

14-6
Enriched detailing derived from the Italian Renaissance. (Windsor)

14-7
A characteristic trait of the mature American Beaux-Arts is this frontispiece entrance composed with paired monumental columns on a rusticated base with enriched and multiple mouldings. (London)

14-8
This square temple building has façades highlighted with engaged Ionic columns with fluted shafts. Note, also, the original window configuration and glazing. (Toronto)

14-9
The monumental arcaded façades are divided by unadorned paired pilasters. Note, also, the half-round Diocletian window located in the attic storey directly above the entrance bay. The glazing is not original. (Thunder Bay)

14–10
This Beaux-Arts style post office building, finished in marble, has a pedimented portico supported by clustered columns in the Composite order. (Owen Sound)

14–11
A dome with fenestrated drum crowns this formal composition inspired by a blend of Georgian and Renaissance architectural detailing. (Brantford)

14−12
This four-columned building inspired by the Greek Doric order has an unusually tall frieze with windows. (Thunder Bay)

14−13
Where the temple form approaches archaeological correctness, size and materials distinguish the early twentieth century Beaux-Arts example from the historic prototype as well as from the more accurate versions of the nineteenth century Classic Revival style. In this case, note how the columns have been spaced to allow a greater distance in the centre for the entrance. The fenestration is also an indication of the early twentieth century date. (Windsor)

14—14
An academic Beaux-Arts example of a six-columned temple plan with acroterion located at the peak and corners of the pediment roof. (Hamilton)

14—15
Beaux-Arts Classicism in scale and composition executed in brick with stone detailing reminiscent of the Colonial Revival. (Sault Ste. Marie)

14—16
An eclectic mixing of styles is very evident in this building, where a
monumental Classical Composite order is supported by a Neo-Gothic style
arched entrance. (Thunder Bay)

14—17
A vernacular interpretation of Beaux-Arts Classicism was popularly adapted for
Carnegie Libraries in many towns across the province.

Chapter 15

Neo-Gothic (1900-1945)

Toronto

Size and the absence of polychromy clearly differentiate this style from the nineteenth century Gothic Revival. The compositional organisation and grandness of design are often likened to Beaux-Arts Classicism, while the decorative details and forms are derived from Gothic prototypes, primarily from the English Perpendicular Gothic and to a lesser extent the Early English Gothic style. Rather than imitate the historical, there is the intention to expand the spatial organization of the earlier Gothic styles. While historical references remain evident in details, the new composition adapts to the different requirements of the twentieth century, resulting in a highly formalized building that is distinguishable from its nineteenth century predecessors by sheer size, the lack of the asymmetrical or picturesque quality, and uniform, almost monochromatic exterior finishes.

The façade of a typical building may be articulated by a series of wall buttresses, too thin for any real structural support, extending upward and even through the cornice or parapet. Large windows may be glazed with traditional tracery or with single panes of glass, in keeping with modern building practices of the early twentieth century. These vertical divisions may be divided horizontally into stories defined by spandrels filled with Gothic low-relief sculpture. The roof, not steep as in the nineteenth century, may not extend above the parapet or cornice, thus stressing the horizontal lines of the building. A squat tower or short turret without spires and occasional finials are the only features piercing the otherwise flat roofline. Stone is the preferred exterior finish, but brick with cut-stone trimming is also used. A veneer of white terra-cotta tiles was often applied to the exterior of commercial buildings and storefronts.

The Toronto architectural firm of Henry Sproatt and Ernest Rolph was influential in establishing the academic prototype of the Neo-Gothic style in Canada. For a brief period Sproatt worked in the office of Cram and Goodhue, the American architects instrumental in spreading this style in the United States and Canada. Well-known examples of the Neo-Gothic style in Ontario by Sproatt and Rolph include Hart House (1911-1919) (see 15-2) and Burwash Hall (1910), both at the University of Toronto.

In spite of the tall chimney stacks, Hart House retains very strong horizontal lines. Cut-stone banding or string courses outline the geometry of the façade, and Gothic detailing is applied around doors and window apertures. The crosslike windows made of stone transoms and mullions with small leaded lights or panes are among those features that are more accurately copied. The great hall annex to the right, with its shallow-pitched roof and large traceried windows filled with coloured glass, is inspired by, but not exactly copied from, the great hall chapels of the English Perpendicular style. Also very characteristic of this style and in contrast to the mature nineteenth century Gothic Revival styles is the richly decorated, spireless square tower. The compound arch entry with smooth-finished archivolts was variously interpreted on many doorways. Based upon this model and others like it at the University of Toronto, the Neo-Gothic style became so widely accepted throughout the Province as the norm for scholastic buildings that "Collegiate Gothic" was aptly coined. In fact, the term also came to be applied to buildings of this style—even though they were not directly associated with formal education—such as churches, chapels and automobile dealerships.

15-1
A formal entrance is marked with a trio of pointed arches crowned with oriel windows. (Windsor)

During the 1930s there were attempts to incorporate Neo-Gothic elements into the mainstream of the then developing Modernist styles. Early high-rise office buildings or skyscrapers were vertically articulated with riblike buttresses and enriched with Gothic-inspired mouldings and details at the street and roof levels. At the extreme, attempts at modernizing the Gothic resulted in buildings with clean surfaces and geometric forms, enhanced by oversimplified Gothic forms, such as acutely pointed windows. At times these elements became so far removed from their Gothic origins that they have more in common with Modern Classicism, where the highly rarified language of the Art Deco style predominates. An example of Modern Gothic is this church in Windsor (see 15—1 and 15—2) with stepped outline, telescopelike tower, angular buttresses and "pointed" apertures.

15—2
A monumental oriel window highlights the frontispiece. (Hart House, University of Toronto, 1911-19, Sproatt and Rolph, architects)

15—3
Hart House at the University of Toronto established an academic example of Neo-Gothic style emulated by numerous colleges and schools (Hart House, University of Toronto, 1911-19, Sproatt and Rolph, architects)

15—4
Smooth stone drip moulds, decorative wall buttresses and a blind arcade frame this arched entrance. (Windsor)

Neo-Gothic (1900-1945)

15—5
A square spireless tower with corner buttresses announces the focal point and entrance of this building. (Toronto)

15—6
Minimalized Gothic and Classical details are uniquely adapted with innovative metal windows having horizontal panes typical of the new materials utilized by the emerging International style. (Windsor)

15—7
15—8
A proliferation of formal Neo-Gothic detailing executed in terra cotta is applied to the framing of this commercial building. (Toronto)

15—9

The wall buttresses and sculptural detail of this Modern Gothic public building more closely approach the very simple forms and lines of Modern Classicism than the richness of the academic Collegiate Gothic examples. (Cochrane)

15—10

This early "high rise" office building has a sparse selection of Neo-Gothic arches, riblike buttresses and sculptural details along the street and roof levels. (Thunder Bay)

15–11
More windows than wall is not uncommon for school buildings. Neo-Gothic detailing is noted along the parapet and around the entrance. (Hamilton)

15–12
Attempts to modernize the Neo-Gothic into the mainstream of modern architecture are well-reflected in this church. Devoid of any additive historical ornament, this example of Modern Gothic has more in common with the forms of the Art Deco and International styles than with Hart House. (Windsor)

Chapter 16 Colonial Revivals (1900-present)

Windsor

While Period Revivals reflect Ontario's European heritage, the Colonial Revivals recall our colonial North American heritage. For just about every European colony established on this continent there developed in the early years of the twentieth century an interest in each colony's architectural past. The most popular was the American Colonial Revival, a hybrid vernacular New England Colonial at times given Beaux-Arts pretentions. The popularity for eighteenth century Colonial architecture of the New England and North Atlantic regions began shortly after the 1876 American Centennial Exhibition, held in Philadelphia, when the New York firm of McKim, Meade and White, who became better known for their Beaux-Arts Classicism, designed "Colonial"-inspired homes for wealthy patrons. Among more humble Anglo American versions are the Early and Late Georgian, the Southern Colonial and the not-so-colonial American Federal. Popular expressions reflecting other colonial powers included the Dutch and the Spanish. In the strictest sense these Colonial styles can be further defined according to their regional location and the period emulated, i.e., Germantown, Pennsylvania Dutch or Ontario Georgian or Loyalist.

In Ontario, architects for the most part accepted the American Revivals with few changes. Attempts were made to include architectural features recalling Loyalist homes of Upper Canada. By the 1930s there was also an effort to incorporate academic and vernacular elements from both English Upper Canada and French Lower Canada with indigenous native characteristics into a unified Canadian National Colonial style. The Runnymede Branch of the Toronto Public Library, designed by John Lyle in 1929 (see 16–1), is an excellent example, with its steep roof, flared eaves, rock-faced stone wall and Classical entrance framed by Indian totems.

The Canadian Centennial (1967) and Ontario Bicentennial (1984) celebrations have recently sparked a renewed concern for our architectural heritage. This has manifested itself not only in the restoration of older buildings but also in the construction of new or Neo-Colonial Revival houses. This time the past includes not only elements from the early Loyalist, English and French traditions, but "Colonial" has been enlarged to include the repertoire of the Classic and Gothic Revivals, as well as the Italianate styles. During the past twenty years, estate subdivision homes have exhibited a mixture of elements not unlike Ontario's eclectic architecture of the mid-nineteenth century: Neoclassical doorways; Classical Revival cornice returns; Gothic pointed windows in centre gables; and corners accentuated with Italianate dichromatic brickwork. Thanks to the newness of construction, the modern materials (snap-on window-glazing bars) and their suburban context with two- or three-car attached garages, there is no doubt as to their place in time.

In general, Colonial Revival buildings, with the exception of accurate museum reproductions, are distinguished from their historic prototypes by the use of modern materials, a different scale or proportional system and a mixture of old and new elements. The inspiration is often based on a broad interpretation of Colonial, and

16–1
Runnymede Branch, Toronto Public Library, Toronto, 1929, John M. Lyle, architect. Notable features of this Canadian National Colonial include:
– steep hip roof with flared eaves
– arched wall dormers
– cornice enriched with abstract Indian motif
– random coursed stone walls
– large-paned, straight-headed sash windows
– frontispiece highlighted with Canadian Indian totemlike enrichments
– smooth-finished stone accentuating dormers, windows and frontispiece

Colonial Revivals (1900-present)

since the selection of parts does not always originate from either a single source or from one identifiable period, the resulting composition is often an eclectic mix of historical architectural details executed with modern or reproduction materials to look old and built to meet twentieth century standards. For example, the end-wall porch or piazza is enclosed to accommodate the automobile, shutters often do not fit the windows they frame and exterior siding is vinyl textured to simulate wood boards. However, when desired, the exactness of historical design and quality of construction can approach museum reproduction standards, making the distinction between the old and new difficult.

16–2
House on Glen Road, Toronto, 1902, Chadwick and Beckett, architects. Notable features of this American Colonial Revival include:
– gambrel roof with pedimented dormers
– modillion block cornice
– monumental pedimented portico in Composite order
– second floor balustraded balcony and Palladian motif
– large entrance with sidelights and generous elliptical fanlight
– glazing pattern that differs from first to second floors
– stone dressings that highlight selected areas around windows
– painted quoins that accentuate corners
– raised stone platform with a balustraded railing
– bay window on end wall

Colonial Revivals (1900-present)

Two examples firmly established the Colonial Revival in Ontario by the first decade of this century. The first, a house designed by the Toronto architectural firm of Chadwick and Beckett (1902), bears a striking resemblance to the Morris House (ca. 1765) in New York City. They both share a monumental portico encompassing a second-floor balcony, but the window glazing, slate roof, contemporary brickwork and stonework and proportions of the Toronto example clearly distinguish the Revival from the Colonial.

The other example, the Central Presbyterian Church in Hamilton, designed in 1907, was among John Lyle's first commissions upon returning from architectural practice in New York City. It is a liberal interpretation of a New England meeting house, executed in smooth brick with academic eighteenth century English Georgian details. Lyle's inventiveness is seen in his ability to extract and translate the essence from Classical prototypes, creating a unique building that significantly departs from traditional Ontario Gothic and Romanesque church designs.

16–3
This formal five-bay centre-hall brick house is highlighted by a typical Georgian entrance, with columns and a swan's neck pediment. The modillion-block cornice, flemish bond brick walls and small window apertures with pronounced keystones all recall the eighteenth century Colonial house of the English Virginia and Maryland colonies. The two-tiered portico on the end wall is a very popular feature of this style. (Windsor)

Colonial Revivals (1900-present)

16—4
This one-and-a-half-storey three-bay brick composition, popular for nineteenth century southern Ontario farmhouses has been adjusted to vernacular twentieth century proportions. The projecting frontispiece is highlighted by a shortened veranda-cum-portico with a Regency-styled tent or awning roof. Tall French-type windows, in fact paired sash windows with an extended apron and through-the-cornice or wall dormers, were relatively rare in colonial times but became very popular features in the Colonial Revival. (Sudbury)

16—5
Characteristics of the Dutch Colonial Revival is the gambrel roof pierced with dormers and a small porch or stoop with benchlike seats. These two houses represent a free or liberal interpretation of the Dutch Colonial. Of particular note is the unique articulation of each roof, one with a one-and-a-half-storey cross gambrel and the other with a pair of tall hip-roofed dormers with a stylized Palladian window. (Thunder Bay)

16–6
Central Presbyterian Church, Hamilton, designed by John Lyle in 1907, is one of the first religious buildings in Ontario to adapt Colonial Revival style.

16–7
An eclectic mixing of Colonial features on a Georgian brick-house form includes: large interior chimneys derived from the eighteenth century vernacular tradition, a denticulated cornice popular with the Classic Revival, the small portico supported by thick columns and the entrance with fanlight belong to the Neoclassical. The ubiquitous Ontario centre gable appears, providing cover for a unique adaptation of the Venetian three-part window. (Cobourg)

Colonial Revivals (1900-present)

16—8
The white painted boards, shuttered multipaned windows topped with a simple moulded cornice, a Classical portico, a panelled entrance door flanked by narrow sidelights, gable roof with end-wall attic windows and an exterior chimney impart the stereotypical modest New England Colonial as seen through twentieth century eyes. (Simcoe)

16—9
An eighteenth century vernacular house form minus the traditional architectural details and enrichments, constructed in the twentieth century. (Sault Ste. Marie)

Variations on the formal eighteenth century American Georgian Colonial is seen in the following:

16–10
Gable roof without dormers. (Cobourg)

16–11
Gable roof with dormers. (Toronto)

16–12
Hip roof with pedimented dormers. (Windsor)

Colonial Revivals (1900-present)

16–13
This unique composition of eclectic but Canadian inspiration is highlighted by a freely adapted Neoclassical door surround and traditional three-part Venetian windows. (Timmins)

16–14
Small clapboard house with massive central chimney. (North Bay)

16—15
The moulded belt course separating the first and second floors mimics the projecting upper floor known in Medieval building terms as a jetty. (Thunder Bay)

16—16
Widely spaced, small multipaned sash windows were a common device used in late eighteenth century vernacular building. (Thunder Bay)

16–17
White painted details, including thin pilaster strips, Venetian windows and an urn-trimmed roof balustrade, provide Neoclassical definition to this highly fenestrated school façade. (Uxbridge)

16–18
This Georgian-inspired public building is exceptional for its red brick and white trim highlighted by a bell tower having a base with coupled pilasters surmounted with balustrade and an open cupola. (Strathroy)

16–19
Modern materials and exaggerated shapes do not hide the inspiration for this interpretation of the Quebec Colonial Revival. (Kirkland Lake)

16–20
A unique Canadian Colonial expression is achieved with a vernacular block-house form trimmed with Classical moulding and crowned by an octagonal cupola. Note, also, the undersized shutters. (South Porcupine)

16—21
This Canadian Colonial is marked by a steeply pitched hip roof, random-coursed stone walls and narrow casement windows recalling not only French-Canadian precedents but also rural architecture of French Normandy. (Toronto)

16—22

The hallmark of the Spanish Colonial Revival is the ever-present broad curvilinear gable. Other characteristics include uniform stucco wall finishes punctuated by round-arched openings and a general lack of surface enrichments. (Windsor)

16—23

Rather than the curvilinear gable, the Pueblo Spanish Colonial style is distinguished by a flat roof with parapets having stucco walls with rounded edges and corners emulating adobe brick. (Sudbury)

Chapter 17 Period Revivals (1900-present)

New Liskeard

Period Revivals in contrast to the Colonial Revivals are inspired not by North American models but by European precedents, primarily English and French.

Most often the English version is loosely modelled after rural cottages and country manor houses of the Tudor period with the occasional high-style Gothic feature, in particular the characteristic Tudor arch. In addition, some Period Revival designs may be marked by a striking combination of Medieval forms with Classical elements reflecting the Elizabethan and Jacobean periods, when Renaissance features began to "modernize" the Gothic. This eclectic blend has often been referred to by the appellation "Jacobethan." The inclusive term "Period Revival" refers to those twentieth century designs that reflect in one way or another this transitional era from the late Gothic or Tudor to the Jacobean periods.

The French counterparts have their prototypes in the late-medieval country houses and manors of Normandy and Brittany. Similar to the English, the French Period Revival reflects vernacular and Classical strains. One shares the Tudor picturesque composition of traditional rural vernacular forms but is distinguished by a round corner tower that serves as both an entrance and stair hall. The materials employed are often similar to the English, but shuttered casement windows and tall hip roofs are preferred. Another variant of the French Period Revival is characterized by a very formal, often symmetrical façade, with Classical detailing restricted to the entrance and window surrounds. Not to be confused with the more complicated Château style, the Period Revival is much simpler in form, not unlike the early English Georgian of the eighteenth century. It is rare to find the tall gabled wall dormer, large cross windows and turrets so characteristic of the Château style. Typically, Period Revival windows are relatively small and segmentally arched, with transomed windows employed occasionally. Double-leaf French-type doors opening onto terraces and patios are also popular.

In Ontario, the most popular of the Period Revivals is a variation on the Tudor Revival house that emulates with certain accuracy of form vernacular building methods and materials. Most noticeable are steeply pitched gable roofs, cross gables and dormers that ideally are covered with shingles simulating a Medieval thatched roof. The ends of gables may be clipped, forming a jerkin-head roof. Stone or brick walls are often combined with a projecting upper floor or jetty. Half-timbering is evident on upper floors, as are narrow casement windows with leaded panes. Window lintels imitating stone or roughly hewn timbers and drip moulds may accentuate openings. The entrance may be highlighted by either

17-1

Notable features of these two academic versions of the Tudor Revival from Hamilton (17-1) and Ottawa (17-2) include:

- *clipped or jerkin-head roof*
- *half-timbered jetty with gable roof*
- *gabled wall dormer*
- *king post and plain vergeboard*
- *brick infill or nogging*
- *exposed rounded wooden pins or treenails*
- *casement windows with leaded panes*
- *plain board drip mould*
- *stone-mullioned and transomed windows*
- *Tudor-arched entrance with compound mouldings*
- *stone hood-mould with label stops*
- *carved spandrels*
- *plank board door*
- *hipped wall dormer*
- *decorated vergeboards*
- *decorated chimney pots*

17-2

Period Revivals (1900-present)

the characteristic Tudor arch or a simple round arch. Less popular elaborate designs based upon more formal manor houses may include not only high-style Gothic details, such as parapet or shaped gables and transomed windows, but numerous Classical elements, including pilaster strips, columns, decorative strap work and stone banding or dressings accentuating corners and window surrounds.

During recent years, Period Revivals have continued to be popular for estate housing developments. Like their contemporary Colonial Revivals, modern materials and a reduced scale or set of proportions distinguish the more recent from the earlier examples.

17–3
Notable features of this academic interpretation of a vernacular medieval English cottage from London, Ontario, include:
- *steep gable roof covered with random coursed multicoloured slates*
- *random coursed rubble stone walls*
- *oriel with diamond-paned casement windows*
- *rough-hewn timber lintel with scalloped profile*
- *modern, industrial-looking metal casement windows*
- *carved vergeboards*
- *half-timbered jetty with projecting beams decorated with carved masks or grotesques*

17—4
A pair of vernaclar variations on the Tudor Revival theme are presented side by side. Each slightly varies the placement of the steep gables and fenestration, but the materials and forms are basically identical. (London)

17—5
This modest brick dwelling is a superb Ontario example of an English vernacular cottage. Most prominent is the steeply pitched cross-gable roof with its highly accentuated or flared peaks. This flared effect is repeated on the roof of the small porch covering the characteristic Tudor-arched entrance. The heavy plank door with iron strap hinges, stepped wall buttresses and narrow sash windows imitating casements complete this twentieth century interpretation. (Thunder Bay)

17–6
A mixture of Late Gothic forms with some Classical elements reflects a vernacular version of the English country house popularly known as the "Jacobethan." The parapet gable with stone trim and casement windows with large mullions appears severe in contrast to the light Classical pilasters framing the entrance door. (Sudbury)

17–7
This simple brick house has been given a Tudor Revival style emphasis with a pair of half-timbered gables facing the street, plain round-arched plank door with iron strap hinges and a pair of rustic lanterns flanking the door. (Sault Ste. Marie)

17—8
*A most definite Tudor Revival style is created in this formal centre-hall plan
with several gables, a projecting half-timbered jetty, an enclosed entrance porch
with a simulated roof truss and large, off-centre chimney. The narrow sash
windows attempt to replicate traditional casements. (Sudbury)*

17—9
*Traditional English Tudor forms, including half-timbered gable, steeply pitched
gable roofs and groupings of narrow windows, are imaginatively composed
with twentieth century materials in these two examples. (Windsor)*

17−10
This eclectic design represents a variety of stylistic characteristics, among them: Queen Anne massing and textures; Gothic Revival half-timbering; and Georgian Classical quoins. (Kingston)

17−11
A commercial application of the vernacular French country house or manoir with Château-style pretentions is expressed in this picturesque composition with miniature corner tower, steep hip roofs with flared eaves, a tall chimney off to one side and narrow casement windows. Respecting the tradition of separating the horses from the manoir, oil companies of the early twentieth century kept their service departments in a detached carriage house. (Toronto)

17–12
A mid-twentieth century simplification of the French manoir is expressed with a mansard roof, slightly arched windows, dormers and pseudo-French-type doors highlighted by a formal entrance with stylized Classical portico. (Sudbury)

17–13
This rambling Medieval-inspired stone house has roll roofing simulating the contours of a traditional thatch roof. (Windsor)

17—14
A Tudor-arched entrance outlined with stone hood-moulds distinguishes this half-timbered frontispiece. (New Liskeard)

17—15
A suggestion of the Tudor Revival is minimally provided in this house, principally as a result of the emphatic application of half-timbering on the upper floors and beneath the gables. (Thunder Bay)

17–16
A streetscape of vernacular-designed English cottages adapted to a Northern Ontario company town. (Iroquois Falls)

17–17
A vernacular application of half-timbering marks the gables of this simple brick house. (Sault Ste. Marie)

Chapter 18 Edwardian Classicism (1900-1930)

North Bay

The simplified but formal composition of the Edwardian house with an emphasis on Classical motifs was indicative of the new direction architecture was to take in the twentieth century. In contrast to the highly colouristic, complicated and often eclectic compositions of the late nineteenth century, Edwardian Classicism, through its balanced façades, simplified but large roofs, smooth brick surfaces and generous fenestration, restored simplicity and order to domestic architecture. It also provided an acceptable forward-looking alternative to the contemporary Period and Colonial Revivals, which looked back to pre-Victorian styles for inspiration and emulation. Generally, the Edwardian façade is highlighted by a frontispiece or portico imaginatively derived from Classical tradition set against a monochromatic smooth exterior brick finish. Tall chimneys are not decorated with enriched terra-cotta panels. Spindles and carved brackets of verandas are minimalized in favour of short colonettes and brick piers. Dormers remained popular, but their profile reflected the simplified shape of the main roof and gone are the profusion of finials and cresting from the ridges. The extended roof eaves are supported not by carved or turned brackets but by plain elongated blocks or cantilevered brackets similar to those used in the Regency and Italian Villa styles. Flat arches made with bricks standing on end or massive but plain stone lintels span apertures. At times, oversized, Classically inspired elements, such as keystone and voussoirs, accentuate window and door surrounds. Contrasting stone trim or dressings may also be used for watertable and string courses. Rather than wood panels, the entrance door often is a full-length panel of clear glass having a bevelled or cut pattern. When stained glass is employed, the designs are simpler and the colours lighter than Victorian examples.

Rather than a profusion of tactile, visual and structural sensations, Edwardian architecture, simply articulated with a selective distribution of strong Classical elements, provided a transitional style from nineteenth century eclecticism to the twentieth century Beaux-Arts Classicism. For instance, the brick façade of the Edwardian office building was generally highlighted by a concentration of stylized and often exaggerated Classical elements. While subdued pilasters and piers were favoured over colossal columns, window surrounds and entrances were often subject to overworked exhibitions of Classical detailing reminiscent of sixteenth century Italian Mannerist architecture. The entrance, enhanced by a variety of elements, columns, pediments and pilasters, often combined or superimposed and linked by heavy rusticated banding, created a surprising, striking and at times even shocking display of architectural virtuosity. The placement of keystones, voussoirs and heavy door enframements take on additional depth in comparison to the otherwise smooth exterior brick finish. The roof of the building is often appropriately finished with a pronounced cornice having large unadorned modillion blocks or cantilever-type brackets.

18—1

Notable features of this academic example from Kingston include:
- *smooth unadorned brick walls with fine joints*
- *large-paned sash windows and rectangular transom with simple pattern*
- *large portico with segmentally arched roof supported by grouped colonettes and shaped cantilever-type brackets*
- *shallow oriel window*
- *flat or jack arch with exaggerated keystone and voussoirs*
- *plain dormers that follow slope of roof*
- *smooth chimneys that provide pilasterlike frames for large end-wall dormers*
- *selective stone dressing for water table, windowsills and lintels*

Edwardian Classicism (1900-1930)

In Ontario, the layering and distortion of motifs was begun during the Classic Revivals of the mid-nineteenth century, most notably in such works as the Don Jail, designed by William Thomas, 1858, and revived in Edwardian Classicism by architects such as G.W. Gouinlock and others. The origins for this inventive handling of Classical elements can be traced through the English Baroque to sixteenth century Italian Mannerism. Much of this highly selective and exuberant display of Classical motifs gave a very distinctive Canadian characteristic to many of the Beaux-Arts designs during the early years of the twentieth century. For commercial buildings the Edwardian characteristic trait of selective but enhanced Classicism was absorbed into the more lavish and monumental successes of the Beaux-Arts. However, the prohibitive costs of Beaux-Arts buildings preserved Edwardian Classicism's popularity for houses well into the 1930s.

18—2
Some notable sixteenth century Mannerist features adapted to Edwardian Classicism seen in this former bank in Thunder Bay include:
— stone channelling or banding of ground-storey walls
— compound window pediments
— rusticated or banded window surrounds
— multiple keystones
— office entrance topped with an enriched mezzanine-level oval window

18-3
Very characteristic of commercial building in the Edwardian Classicism style is the selective but striking and heavy handling of the Classical elements in sharp contrast with the smooth brick exterior. Multiple mouldings banded by large blocks and oversized keystone are motifs ultimately derived from sixteenth century Italian Mannerism. (Factory building, Toronto, 1905, G.W. Gouinlock, architect)

18-4
This frontispiece is a typical Edwardian motif that found popularity in the more baroque version of Beaux-Arts Classicism. Of particular note are the emphatic keystones and voussoirs of the windows. Note, also, the brick banding or channelling along the ground level. (Factory building, Toronto, 1901, G.W. Gouinlock and Baker, architects)

18-5
Edwardian Classicism's preference for abstraction and Classical refinement are well represented in this arcaded brick wall. Every fifth row of bricks is recessed, forming a channelled or banded effect that continues uninterrupted, wrapping around each pilaster, forming radiating voussoirs for the arched window, then repeating that pattern for each bay. The pilasters are given minimal accents and the architrave above is reduced to a series of thin mouldings complementing the banding below. The window glazing is late twentieth century. (Pembroke)

18—6
The exaggeration of select architectural details on this corner bank building becomes an easily recognizable hallmark of Edwardian Classicism. (Toronto)

18—7
The sharply delineated cornice, contrasting keystones, voussoirs and the columned frontispiece are executed with the pronounced clarity characteristic of Edwardian Classicism. (North Bay)

18-8
The contrast between Edwardian and Beaux-Arts Classicism is subtly blended in this vernacular expression. (Hawkesbury)

18-9
An abstract design of emulated Classical details with contrasting brick, stone trim and emphatic linear roof dominates the composition of this apartment building. (Toronto)

Edwardian Classicism (1900-1930)

Half columns or colonnettes of various and imaginative profiles highlight these examples:

18−10 Plain Tuscan. (Georgetown)

18−11 Fluted Corinthian. (Dundas)

18−12 Unique "bowling pin" shape. (Peterborough)

172

Surviving Queen Anne forms and textures are mixed with selective Edwardian features:

18–13 Oval windows with not one but four oversized keystones. (Ottawa)

18–14 Select stone accents (Erin)

18–15 Ceramic hanging tiles. (Sault Ste. Marie)

Edwardian Classicism (1900-1930)

18—16
Straight stone window accents, half columns and plain roof eaves mark this modest square variant of Edwardian Classicism. (Georgetown)

18—17
A unique and vernacular twist is given to this concrete block house with large paired cornice brackets and paired half-columns. (Cornwall)

18—18
Edwardian Classicism taken to extreme simplicity is represented in this vernacular-design double house with contrasting window lintels set against smooth brick walls, tapered and squared porch piers raised on brick pedestals and a parapet cornice with abstracted pediment. (Cornwall)

174

Devoid of obvious Classical detailing, these houses represent a transition from the Edwardian to the more modern, less historical compositions leading to the Prairie and Craftsmen styles:

18–19, Hamilton.

18–20, Dundas.

18–21, Brampton.

Chapter 19 Bungalow (1900-1945)

Grimsby

In the strictest sense, "Bungalow" refers to any one-storey dwelling built for seasonal or temporary use. In nineteenth century India the term referred to a low one-storey house surrounded by a veranda and used as an inn for travellers. During the early years of this century in California, the Bungalow became more than a temporary cottage or cabin. The Bungalow style is a permanent home maintaining in many instances the appearance of a one-storey house, with sleeping quarters often squeezed into the upper floor; in more fully developed or elaborate examples a full second storey is concealed beneath the overhanging roof.

By 1911, Bungalow living had become so popular in the United States that Henry Saylor wrote the landmark book *Bungalows*; a second edition published in Toronto appeared in 1913. In this book he defines and illustrates ten types of Bungalows, from the simple seasonal "tent house" to the formal two-storey permanent house that "looks like" a Bungalow. In addition, plans for Bungalows appeared in many home magazines through the twenties and thirties, assuring their popularity until the advent of the Second World War.

The broad, gently pitched roof, extensive porches or verandas in an informal asymmetrical plan combined with a variety of building materials, with no applied ornamentation, are characteristic of the style. As Saylor writes: "…and in order to secure that blanket-like roof that is associated with the true bungalow type, the main roof or its gables will usually cover the porch space as well as the interior with a minimum number of breaks." Thus one roof covers not only verandas, but sunroom and sleeping porches, and generally extends well beyond the walls of the house, terminating in deep overhanging eaves. In some instances the amount of covered exterior space may exceed the square footage of usable interior room. When large cross gables or dormers are employed their slope or pitch is similar to the main roof.

Another favourite feature shared with some examples of the Gothic Revival is exposed structural framing. Purlins, rafters, plates, braces and posts are highly visible in gable ends, under eaves, as well as supporting members for the extensive porches and verandas. Building materials varied, but most favoured was the combining of rustic textures, such as stone or brick with a siding, such as horizontal board or shingle. At least one chimney, usually large, in stone or brick, can be found along a wall or centrally located along the slope of the roof. Windows are often grouped in twos or threes and may be multipaned or single. Diamond-paned casements are also employed.

A prime example of the open-plan California-inspired Bungalow is the house in Grimsby (see 19–2). Characteristic features include lack of applied ornament, exposed structural members and a veranda with ladderlike frieze comprised of large beams having short intermediate posts or braces. Rounded stones, some approaching boulderlike proportions, used for walls, form inverted arches supporting the extensive roof. A raised centre section to accommodate sleeping areas created a unique profile that was popularly dubbed the "aeroplane" design. This unique profile was also shared with some Prairie-style examples. Like the Prairie style, the aesthetic appeal of these houses relied not so much on applied decoration but on an informal composition with strong horizontal rooflines and openness of plan executed with rustic and natural-appearing materials.

19–1
A California Bungalow from Construction, *April 1912.*

However, much like the Octagon style that preceded it, the Bungalow was often subject to a variety of add-on stylistic features (see 19–19 and 19–20). Some eclectic additions include: Tudor arches, undersized Palladian windows and Spanish-inspired red pantile-covered roofs. Nonetheless, Bungalow characteristics prevail, i.e., low, one-storey, ground-hugging expansive profile with gently pitched gable roofs and exposed structural roof members.

19–2
The outline of this Bungalow with extensive verandas, raised central sleeping area and exposed structural roof members is similar to the illustrated California bungalow. (Grimsby)

19–3
Aptly named Boulder Villa, this Bungalow is closely patterned after the Grimsby example. (Boulder Villa, ca. 1929, Clarkson, Mississauga)

19-4
19-5
These two vernacular variations of the California Bungalow are situated near each other. (Essex County).

19-6
Stressing the load-bearing capacity of beams to their full potential resulted in open, spacious full-width verandas. (Toronto)

Bungalow (1900-1945)

While from the street many Bungalows appear to be modest dwellings, the side elevations reveal two and even three floors of living space. (19—7, Brampton;19—8, Wellington; 19—9, Leamington; 19—10, Thunder Bay; and 19—11, Petrolia)

19—7

19—8

19—9

19—10

19—11

19—12
A street of Bungalows provides a
unifying scale while also allowing for
considerable individual variations in
colour, materials and details. (Windsor)

Bungalow (1900-1945)

While not elaborate in composition, these Bungalow-styled cottages suited to smaller budgets are noted for simplicity of construction, lack of applied ornament, enclosed sun porches and a pergola. (19−13, Thunder Bay; 19−14, Kirkland Lake; 19−15, Windsor; 19−16, Cobourg and 19−17, Thunder Bay).

19−13

19−14

19−15

19–16

19–17

Bungalow (1900-1945)

The following are unique variations of the Bungalow Style: an emphatic two-storey elevation (19–18 Windsor), a Japanese pagoda-style roof (19–19 Thunder Bay), and a Colonial Revival with Tuscan-Styled columns. (19–20 Haileybury)

19–18

19–19

19–20

Chapter 20 Prairie (1910-1930)

Dwyer Hill

The Prairie style, originating in the midwestern United States, had a strong horizontal character, heightened by long, gently pitched rooflines and other linear elements complementing the flatness and openness of the prairies, thus giving the style its regional appellation. The style matured under the leadership of Frank Lloyd Wright and his associates during the early years of this century. The designs emanating from Wright's Oak Park, Illinois, studio were endowed with geometric qualities, including not only strong horizontals, but rectangles, squares and verticals, as well. Prairie style samples are marked by a frank use of materials and definite absence of historical ornament. Rather than relying on either Classic or Gothic historical detail, aesthetic form became a natural result of the "organic growth" or arrangement of structure and materials consistent with a geographic area. The plan and elevation were thought out from a functional perspective without benefit of any preconceived image of what the house should look like. When ornament was used, it continued the "organic" concept, with either curvilinear, florid, "Art-Nouveau" patterns reminiscent of designs by Wright's teacher and mentor, Louis Sullivan, or the decorative elements assumed geometric shapes, at times having a rustic quality reminiscent of the "arts and crafts" forms that were very much publicized in such journals as the American magazine *The Craftsman*. Similar geometric motifs also appear in the Bungalow, Edwardian and even Neo-Gothic styles. Wright himself continued to develop "organic architecture" in very personal directions while others adapted his principles and the Prairie style to various parts of North America.

The Prairie style was brought to Canada by Francis C. Sullivan (no relation to Louis), who, after having apprenticed to F. L. Wright, returned to his native Ontario to establish his architectural practice in Ottawa. The large expansive houses more typical of the American Midwest were never realized on such scale in this country. However, Sullivan designed a number of buildings that clearly reflect Wright's influence. Exercising a very personal interpretation, Sullivan adapted the Prairie style and Craftsman decorative detailing to the Ontario context. Sullivan's designs are hallmarked by stark geometric forms that in and of themselves possess little aesthetic value, but when combined create spatial depth, texture and colour. The cubic mass or squareness of a typical design is marked by a continuous stone foundation sill, continuous string course or band of dark-stained wood delineating a shortened horizontal second-storey level, and square roof cornice with wide unsupported eaves. Plain horizontal stone trimming or bands may terminate a chimney or corner piers. Geometric glazing patterns repeated in all windows complement the rectilinear quality of the house. Also typical is the use of plain boards, not only for accent strips, but also for windows and door trim. Often windows of the narrow casement variety are grouped in twos or threes and, defying traditional construction techniques, are sometimes placed at corners.

The Conners House in Ottawa, built from 1914 to 1915, represents Sullivan's finest extant example of a Prairie-style residence, even though there remains an apparent concession to Ontario's traditional building forms, i.e., the tall gable roof and end-wall chim-

20-1
Noteworthy features of this Prairie-style house in Ottawa include:
- *continuous stone sill*
- *string courses of dark-stained wood bands*
- *a shortened second-storey level*
- *horizontal or all-stretcher brick bond*
- *square roof cornice*
- *unsupported eaves*
- *geometric window glazing*

20–2
While lacking some of the finishes and details of the Conners House, this vernacular version shares the shortened second storey and the overall shape and proportion of the Conners House. (Brampton)

neys. There is, however, no doubt that the bold geometric and unadorned composition reflects Sullivan's appreciation of Wright's concepts as expressed in the Prairie style. The horizontal characteristic so typical of the ideal Prairie style has much of its strength diluted in Ontario by Sullivan's personal preference for strong vertical accents, such as the large projecting corner piers, heavy brick porch supports and tall chimneys. One's initial reaction to this unconventional geometric composition of the Conners House is that if it were not for the massive chimneys anchoring the roof and walls, the roof would either fly off or would slide down the chimney sides, crushing the urns, and reduce the house by one storey. However, the Prairie style had no rigid dogma, no strict rules or technical pattern books to follow, thus allowing liberal interpretations of Wright's original concept of "organic flow or growth," so that no two houses were ever identical.

When compared to other then current architectural styles, Sullivan's buildings are indeed very avant-garde, and have much in common with modern architectural trends, not only in the United States, but in Europe, as well. The most obvious recognizable traits shared by Sullivan and his European contemporaries pioneering the International style include a strong preference for geometric shapes and the abhorrence of historically derivative ornament. There are no Classical or Gothic mouldings and enrichments.

Prairie (1910-1930)

20-3
Rather than placing supporting posts at each corner, the architect has inserted innovative corner windows, which when combined with the geometric composition and lack of applied historical ornament create a very modern look to this early twentieth century house. (Ottawa, F. C. Sullivan, architect)

20-4
Wide unsupported eaves, square cornice and flat roofs extending from a taller central block create the profile that led to the "aeroplane" designation for many Prairie- and Bungalow-style buildings. (Horticultural Building, Lansdowne Park, 1914, F. C. Sullivan, architect)

20-5
One of the few examples of a Prairie-style building exhibiting not only panels with low-relief curvilinear sculpture but geometric "orders" decorating windows and doors. (Library, Pembroke, 1911, F. C. Sullivan, architect)

20–6
Georgian traditions die hard, as do Prairie-style concepts, as evidenced in the shape and proportion of this house, with its low-pitched hip roof, wide unsupported eaves, grouping of casement-type windows and the shortened second storey delineated by a continous horizontal contrasting band. The horizontal emphasis is continued by maintaining the same roof profile for the front porch and projecting side bay. (House, Simcoe, 1962, W. M. Smale, architect, originally designed as a convent for St. Mary's Roman Catholic Church)

20–7
The emphasis on geometry, with flat roof, deep eaves with square cornice, grouping of casement windows and strong corner piers, is very characteristic of the Ontario Prairie style. A Craftsman-style detail popular with other early twentieth century modern styles is the turned square-on-square motif visible on each corner pier. (House, ca. 1910, Toronto)

Prairie (1910-1930)

20-8
The Ontario vernacular preference for the vertical is expressed in the massive corner piers and gable roof. The combination smooth brick and rough-cast stucco is also typical. Craftsmanlike qualities are evident in the stained glass and in the square panel on each pier. The ribbed concrete streetlight with a similar textured finish is highlighted with a variation on the geometric "capital" seen on the Pembroke Library. (House, Ottawa)

20-9
Abstractions of Classical and Craftsman motifs appear side by side on this transitional Prairie-style school; stylized cornice brackets have been placed under the deep roof eaves, geometric panels in contrasting materials decorate wall surfaces and the entrance is treated with a minimal pediment and pilasters decorated with squares. (St. George's School, Windsor)

20—10

20—11
The geometric and linear qualities of this Prairie style church are evident in the bell tower and window glazing, and are contrasted with a traditional gable roof. (Dwyer Hill)

20—12
This freely interpreted vernacular Prairie style has strong horizontal qualities expressed through cantilevered roof and balcony, bands of windows and a flat-roofed entrance canopy framed by a pair of strong vertical accents. (Brockville)

Chapter 21 Art Deco (1925-1940)

Toronto

Highly decorative, colouristic and abstract, this style reached its zenith shortly after the 1925 "Exposition des arts décoratifs" held in Paris, from which it acquired its popular name and image. As exhibited in Paris, this style was applied to all the decorative arts, from graphic design to furniture to jewelry, and strongly influenced architectural design, as well. Characterized by a lavish and exotic application of materials with angular outlines, Art Deco motifs acquired inspiration from ancient Egyptian artifacts, Pre-Columbian Indian designs and more contemporaneous influences, such as the Cubist and Fauvist painters. Complete with "jazzy" and up-to-date elements, but not turning a blind eye to historicism, Art Deco found an immediate audience among the wealthy, who could afford high fashion, interior designers and personal architects. After the economic crash of 1929, the rage for Art Deco continued, but on a more pragmatic and popular level.

21−1
Characteristic of the Art Deco style applied to an asymmetrical composition recalling early examples of the International style is this small movie theatre, enhanced with angular lincs, brick banding, panels of coloured glass and metal trim. (Timmins)

Art Deco (1925-1940)

21-2
Predating the soaring International style steel-and-glass super high rise of the 1960s are examples, such as this Art Deco-style skyscraper, with clean vertical accents expressed in brick with spinelike buttresses turned forty-five degrees, presenting a sharp edge to the street. The columns of windows continue the upward thrust with spandrels decorated with vertical grooves or channels. As is typical of early skyscrapers, the enriched decoration can be found on the parapet, which in this case is treated with multicoloured abstract motifs. (Toronto)

Architecturally, in Ontario, Art Deco is noted primarily for decorative ornament on buildings exhibiting Modernist influences seen most often on early examples of the International and streamlined Art Moderne styles. At times buildings having predominately Classical or Neo-Gothic characteristics may adapt Art Deco-style decorative details and ornament. Features, such as capitals and pilasters of the Classical orders, may be so abstracted or stylized that their appearance is but a shadow of what they originally represented. Early skyscrapers having a series of setbacks or stepped profile with strong vertical accents are often highlighted with Art Deco motifs, including colourful tiles around the entrance and at street levels, as well as along the cornices or parapets. Between the street and roof levels, spandrels connecting vertical strips of windows may be enriched with low-relief ornament depicting stylized birds or flowers combined with geometric zigzags or waves. Window apertures are predominately straight and may be acutely pointed, but, when a round shape is desired, ideally the angular octagon is preferred.

Art Deco (1925-1940)

21–3
The hard-edged, low-relief sculptured pyramidlike forms of these metal spandrels are complemented by the geometry of two-toned brick banding on the lower or street level. (Toronto)

21–4
An abstraction of decorative detailing, including water and floral motifs, is evident in the low-relief sculptural motifs found around these lower floor windows. Note the metal-framed windows that are often used on early twentieth century examples of buildings influenced by Modernism. (Toronto)

21–5
Simple brick bands creating a linear effect combined with the angular sawtooth cornice moulding and abstracted corner finial with stepped profile are vernacular Art Deco features applied to a small commercial building. (Kirkland Lake)

21—6
Art Deco-style detailing applied to Classical motifs enhances this automobile service garage entrance. The pilasters framing the door are terminated by stepped finials treated with a geometric starburstlike capital. An angular quality is continued in the centre vertical moulding, which is laterally reinforced along the parapet by a pair of squared scroll brackets. Octagonal panels are enriched with low-relief sculpted birds, celestial bodies and water motifs. (Toronto)

21—7   21—8
An elaborate and rich example of Art Deco style detailing is evident in this floriated metal panel. Modern Classicism is also suggested by the formal symmetry of the façade framed by "fluted pilasters." Note, also, the favoured Art Deco octagonal form for the projecting clock. (Toronto)

Art Deco (1925-1940)

21-9
A vernacular interpretation of Modern Classicism with Art Deco subtleties. (South Porcupine)

21-10
The multiple corners, geometric mouldings and angularity create an Art Deco abstraction of a pedimented Classical entrance. A concession to traditional design is the natural-appearing cartouche or crest. (London)

Art Deco stylization of Gothic ornament enhances the upper reaches of these two early skyscraper office buildings. (21-11, Thunder Bay; 21-12, Windsor)

21−13
The stepped-back configuration emphasized with flat roofs, straight apertures,
lack of enrichments and the octagonal lanterns are characteristic of Art Deco,
but the rock-faced stone and the multipaned wood sash windows are
appropriate to the Colonial and Château styles. (Georgetown)

21−14
Geometric floral motifs highlight the decorative stone accents of this modest
apartment building.

Chapter 22

Art Moderne (1930-1945)

Toronto

During the 1930s, the hard edge of Art Deco style and the Cubist-like compositions of the Bauhaus-influenced prewar Early International style were modified by industrial design influences. Indication of this change in modern design was evidenced at two world's fairs. The first was Chicago's Century of Progress Exposition in 1934, where among the futuristic exhibits were a new streamlined train, a circular house of tomorrow, a building made entirely of glass blocks and Buckminster Fuller's inventive Dymaxion Car. The other was the New York World's Fair of 1939, which had several innovative buildings. The pavilions of Great Britain and Denmark were particularly representative, with their sweeping horizontality, rounded corners and long continuous bands of windows. The new designs of this period have been variously referred to as "Depression Modern," "Horizontal Deco," "Streamlined Moderne" or simply "Modernistic." The present appellation recognizes the architects' involvement with art of architecture and industrial design, as well as the desire to incorporate the most up-to-date, streamlined and French "moderne" look into North American design and building.

Innovative in its application of the latest industrial design concepts and maintaining a disdain for historicism, Art Moderne stands in sharp contrast to the highly ornamentive and colouristic designs of Art Deco. Rather than the vertical and angular accents of Art Deco, Art Moderne preferred to emphasize fluidity of the "streamlined." This is achieved with horizontal effects, rounded corners, smooth wall surfaces, flat roofs and continuous string courses that heighten the visual length of the design. Selected large expanses of glass were employed, curving or wrapping around corners or along bowed bays. Round windows and translucent glass blocks were also popular. The inclusion of a cornice or any other traditional historical detail was an absolute taboo, shared in common with Modernism in general and the International style. Polished metals such as stainless steel were used sparingly for handrails and accent trim. Commercial buildings, particularly storefronts, highway diners and auto garages, often exhibited polished metals, enameled panels and neon advertisement, at times mixed with Art Deco style ornament.

In Ontario houses, Art Moderne features, such as rounded corners and translucent glass blocks, are commonly seen side by side with some selective Art Deco abstract decorative ornament on an otherwise typical Cubist composition in the prewar Early International style.

The following Art Moderne-style houses reflect characteristics very similar to the Early International and Art Deco styles, but are distinguished by streamlined forms, including curved bays, circular towers and rounded corners that generally result in a more horizontal composition than the Cubist and stepped compositions of the other Modernist styles.

22–1
Note the horizontal windowpanes, narrow vertical stair hall light, smooth wall finish and flat roof with plain metal flashing. (Hamilton)

22–2
This example is similar in form to 22-1, but with sash corner windows rather than the casement type and a curved corner filled with a monumental wraparound window. Note, also, the concession to tradition with the blocklike cornice moulding. (Tweed)

22—3
A tall stair hall filled with glass blocks and a portico with streamlined corners highlight this example. (Ottawa)

22—4
Rounded corners, bowed window, balconies and rooftop metal railings distinguish this house. Note, also, the horizontal windowpanes. (Toronto)

22–5
A stepped composition, with rounded ends and rooftop terrace and lookout, creates a streamlined effect reminiscent of a ship's bridge. (Burlington)

22–6
Modernist styles are uniquely combined in this railway station. Streamlined Art Moderne influences are seen in the round forms at the corners and entrances and in the smooth exterior stone finish, while the profile of the entire composition, with its stepped office tower, large corner windows and vertical strip of windows centred above the main entrance, heightens the Cubist qualities familiar to the Art Deco and Early International styles. (Hamilton, former Toronto, Hamilton and Buffalo Railway System)

22–7
A monumental four-storey silolike shaft or tower with a triad of continuous vertical strips of glass blocks highlights the façade of this vernacular interpretation of Modernism. Note, also, the mock corner windows with horizontal panes. (Ottawa)

22–8
Streamlined Art Moderne forms are uniquely adapted with a variety of circular shapes and textured finishes for a movie theatre. (Thunder Bay)

22–9
Vernacular streamlining is succinctly captured in this Art Moderne-style "boomtown" commercial front. (Iroquois Falls)

22–10
A vernacular mix of decorative brickwork reminiscent of the Art Deco style is blended with rounded corners and an uninterrupted roof that are associated with the Art Moderne style. (London)

Art Moderne (1930-1945)

22-11
The bold graphics above the curved corner entrance accurately reflect the Modernist intentions of this building emphasized with multiple rounded forms and a smooth, exterior wall finish. (Timmins)

22-12
A simple blending of Art Deco forms with Art Moderne shapes is evident in the stepped profile of the entrance, rounded corner with wraparound glass blocks and circular canopy cantilevered over the basement entrance. (Sarnia)

22-13
A futuristic tower with industrial finlike buttresses combined with a sweeping façade creates an easily identifiable landmark. (Sault Ste. Marie)

Chapter 23 International (1930-65)

Ottawa

The name of this style was first used in conjunction with the 1932 Museum of Modern Art's exhibition in New York City entitled "The International Style: Architecture since 1922." This exhibit brought together for the first time examples of works by many architects from various parts of the world. Thus this cosmopolitan partiality, combined with the group's forward-looking modern architectural ideas, predicated the adoption of the exhibition's title, International.

Modernism is the larger, more encompassing design concept that gave birth to several Modernist styles, including the International. While the roots of this style lie in the nineteenth century, Modernism with a capital M did not take practical form and cohesiveness as a movement until the 1920s at the Bauhaus School in Germany. Under the direction of Walter Gropius and later Mies van der Rohe, artists, designers, craftsmen and architects from all over Europe worked as teams to "build the future."

Central to the Modernist's vision was the rejection of the imitative copying of past historical styles. Rather than applying historicism to enrich machine production, the Bauhaus School sought to express the intrinsic values and beauty inherent in the new materials and new technology of the twentieth century. Everything from teapots to buildings was designed to fit this new forward-thinking creed. It was also believed that standardization was a natural part and a result of the greater design process, bringing functional and beautiful objects within the economic means of the greatest number of people. The finished products often shared a constructive or industrial image. This functional expression of construction and materials, devoid of historically derived ornament, became a hallmark of Modernist design. The limited practical application of Modernist principles in Europe as taught at the Bauhaus School was briefly halted by the unfavourable political climate of Nazi Germany. Gropius, Mies van der Rohe and other pioneers of modern design associated with the Bauhaus School fled to England and America, where they continued to develop their concepts and ideas and to instruct another generation, whose opportunity to build would come after the Second World War.

Strongly influenced by the Bauhaus School and building precedents in prewar England, Ontario examples of the Early International style are characterized by simple Cubist compositions, with flat roof, clean lines, straight edges and smooth exterior finishes, usually punctuated by small windows. Besides the flat roof, the most outstanding characteristic is the absolute absence of applied historical ornament. The functional expression of new construction techniques and materials is more evident on industrial and utilitarian structures rather than on private dwellings and public buildings. Generally, window apertures are filled with multipaned steel-framed windows that may continue around corners. Ideally, whether steel- or wood-framed, the individual windowpanes are placed on a horizontal axis rather than the traditional vertical. The corner window, which was used in some examples of the Prairie style, is also popular. The complete elimination of the conventional load-bearing wall in favour of the monolithic but transparent glass curtain wall was not fully applied until after 1950.

Two examples of the Early International style, with flat roof, Cubist composition and, irregular placement of windows, built-in garage, are well-represented in the April and August 1936 issues of the *JRAIC* (see 23−1 and 23−2). Further, the brick or concrete block wall of the illustrated house was finished with stucco, "…presenting an overall clean, smooth surface," as was recommended in *The Modern House in England*, published in 1937. At times a rounded

23−1
"An Example of Modern Domestic Architecture" from the April 1936 issue of the **Journal of the Royal Architectural Institute of Canada.** *(Metropolitan Toronto Reference Library)*

corner or bay adds a streamlined effect, recalling the Art Moderne, and angular Art Deco abstract detailing may highlight other parts of the façade. An excellent Canadian version of the Early International style is Highfields, a country residence designed in 1936 by the architect John Lyle for his own use (see 23–3). Although the house was never built, the design combines the Modernist's asymmetrical Cubist composition, smooth wall finishes and flat roofs with a traditional central focus in the form of a tall rounded projecting frontispiece embellished with a sculpted crest, a formal composition device reflecting Lyle's Beaux-Arts academic training and adapted for many vernacular International-style homes.

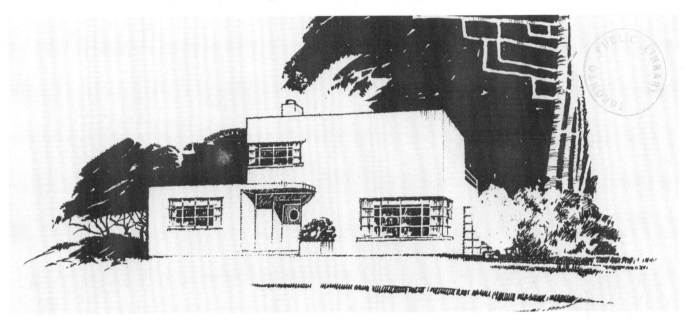

23–2
Ontario Government Small House Competition entry from the August 1936 issue of the Journal of the Royal Architectural Institute of Canada.
(Metropolitan Toronto Public Library)

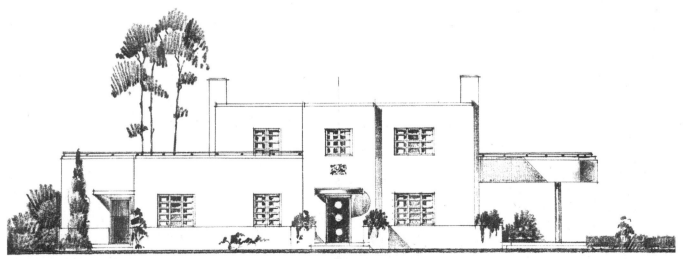

·NORTH·ELEVATION·

23–3
North elevation of John Lyle's proposed country residence, Highfields. (Ontario Public Archives)

International (1930-1965)

23−4
An excellent example of the Early International style that could have been modelled after one of the entries in the Small House Competitions illustrated in the JRAIC of 1936. Very characteristic is the Cubist composition, flat roofs, steel-framed corner windows, roof decks, smooth monochromatic finish and a complete lack of any applied ornament, either abstract or historical. (Simcoe)

23−5
This square composition is enhanced with a corner tower crowned by a penthouse and rooftop deck. An element of tradition is alluded to with a cornicelike moulding. The sliding glass door is a recent alteration. (Hamilton)

23−6
A simplified Cubist composition having a mildly corbelled cornice is enhanced with an asymmetrical arrangement of apertures and smooth brick walls; a curved wall adds a streamlined quality to the entrance. (Timmins)

23-7
Decorative banding and octagonal windows are elements popular with the Art Deco style. (North Bay)

23-8
Characteristic features of this formal-appearing Early International building include the flat roof, thin vertical stair hall light, horizontal paned windows, monochromatic exterior finish and the lack of applied historical ornament. (Port Credit, Mississauga)

23-9
The typical Cubist composition in this case is lightened by a large expanse of ground-floor windows comprised of many small panes of glass. (Sault Ste. Marie)

Fuelled by the building boom, the renewed availability of materials and a profound optimism in Modernist design principles, the International style blossomed during the 1950s. As a teacher at the Illinois Institute of Technology and by his practical examples, Mies van der Rohe was instrumental in formulating a mature International style. Highly refined and regulated, the ideal expression of construction and materials is so closely associated with Mies's design idiom "less is more" that this pinnacle of Modernism is often referred to as Miesian Modern or Miesian International. Essentially, buildings in this style, characterized by a minimalist approach, are completely devoid of historical ornament. The precise edges and structural clarity utilize the simplest but highest-quality materials and finishes available.

Whether a high-rise office building, such as Toronto's T-D Centre, 1963-67, by Mies and the Canadian firm of John B. Parkin and Associates, or a small private house, such as Hart Massey House, Ottawa, 1959, façades are marked by a structural nakedness and visual openness. Ideally, exposed steel beams provide a grid frame that is filled with curtains preferably of glass or a combination of glass with wood, metal or brick panels. In some buildings, the entire steel-and-glass box may be lifted above ground, achieving an illusionary "free-floating" effect. At times this effect is exaggerated by raising the body of the building on pillars known as "pilotis." In the example of the T-D Centre, the base is visually an open cage of monolithic sheets of plate glass with revolving glass doors along the base. Above this base or lobby level, metal mullions, securing the curtain wall of glass, soar skyward uninterrupted to the flat rooftop. Along the interior of the lobby, several

23–10
The Miesian International Style applied to a small house is characterized by a structure of exposed steel framing resulting in some open grids and others enclosed with wood panels. (Hart Massey, architect, Rockcliffe Park, Ottawa)

23–11
In the mature Miesian International style, giant "pilotis" or feet of the superstructure allow for an expansive glass-enclosed lobby where smaller I beams, not part of the main supporting structural system, secure the curtain walls of windows and spandrels. (T-D Centre, Toronto)

large blocklike piers enclosed with highly polished stone provide elements of mass and solidity that visually anchor the building to the ground, implying more than simply clothing for the elevators.

The rapid growth of these steel-and-glass compositions was largely due to the facility with which the basic grid or module could be repeated. In fact, the belief that good modern design could be and should be copied encouraged the adoption of the Miesian model. In many instances reinforced concrete substituted for the steel frame. The Miesian International style quickly became the most sought-after expression for high-rise commercial building during the mid-twentieth century. However, by the end of the 1960s, the emulation of Miesian prototypes became either overly personalized or so rigidly formalized as to be monotonous. In the hands of the less talented the design creed "less is more" gave way to a "least is best" approach, lost public interest and only temporarily provided corporate patrons with the tallest building for the lowest price per square foot. Only the laws of mechanics and zoning limited the height and size of these sophisticated well-engineered buildings. During the 1960s and 1970s, buildings were often marked by exaggerated structural expressions or individually patterned decorative elements. These Late Modern and Decorated Modern variants provided the background for the next major change in architecture.

23–12
The typical Cubist composition of the Early International style is continued while adapting to more recent Contempo-style advances in glass and steel in this split-level 1950s house. (Sudbury)

23–13
This hydro substation is eclectically enhanced with a large bank of windows, a rounded tower and circular window reminiscent of the Art Moderne and an Art Deco low-relief sculpture in the panel above the entrance. (Windsor)

23–14
A liberal interpretation of early Modernist design concepts executed with post-1950s materials. (Stoney Creek)

23–15
A traditional house plan with hip roof, gabled frontispiece and textured Period Revival brick walls is provided with a hint of vernacular Modernism with horizontal-paned windows and clean unadorned mouldings. (Thunder Bay)

23–16
A stepped-back façade, accent bands, corner windows, steel-framed casements and smooth stucco exterior finish provide a vernacular blend of Art Deco and International style elements. (Simcoe)

23–17
Whether or not the pebble dash second floor was planned in the original design, the result is emphatically a vernacular interpretation of the Early International style. (Ottawa)

23–18
A blending of European Bauhaus Modernist features with those emanating from the American Midwest and the Pacific Coast can be seen in the following, where monochromatic exterior finishes have been replaced by materials rendered in a more natural fashion and the Cubist composition is reduced to a series of horizontals with deep overhanging roofs more in keeping with the earlier Prairie style. Wood siding and rock-faced stonework are incorporated with International style features, including flat roofs, corner windows and sunscreens, and, of course, the taboo against applied ornament remains respected. Sharing a spirit similar to those designs by Gropius and Breuer during the late 1930s, these Ontario examples from the 1940s are preludes to the Contempo style of the 1950s.

23-19
Toronto.

23-20
A diminutive T-D Centre is expressed in this office building. (Kingston)

23-21
The hard-edged, linear, boxlike skeletal forms of Miesian prototypes are enhanced with brick-filled panels and coloured aprons or spandrels. Note, also, how the steel frame is slightly raised above ground on miniature "pilotis," creating an illusionary "free-floating" effect similar to Mies's landmark Farnesworth House, 1950, in Illinois. (Toronto)

23-22
The "pilotis" in this case are encased with stone, and the upper-floor curtain wall cantilevered and secured by highly polished aluminum mullions. (Windsor)

23—23
Polished black marble heightens the vertical emphasis of this low-rise International-style building executed in concrete rather than steel. (City Hall, Sarnia)

23—24
This apartment block takes advantage of widely spaced concrete piers or "pilotis" to allow for a car park. Note, also, the pedestallike steel column supporting the projecting terrace and boxlike entrance. (Sudbury)

23–25
While the mature Miesian examples generally expressed a vertical orientation, other versions of the International style included buildings with strong horizontal forms that still achieved considerable height. This building prefers an almost streamlined Art Moderne look with bands of channelled concrete "walls" separated by continuous ribbons of small-paned windows. (Toronto)

23–26
By the 1980s, the application of the curtain wall is taken to the extreme in this Late Modern example with reflective glass panels rising directly from the sidewalk, visually defying the traditional supporting piers or "pilotis" of the International style. (Toronto)

Chapter 24　Victory Housing (1940-50)

Peterborough

During the 1940s, the federal government attempted to meet the growing demand for low-cost rental accommodation for employees of defence-related industries and returning war veterans. One programme administered by War Time Housing Ltd., a crown corporation, was responsible for assisting municipalities with temporary rental housing for employees–their families included–who worked in nearby munitions plants, assembly lines and other military-related activities supporting the victory effort. In some instances, entire communities were established, with detached houses for families and social support service buildings, such as community centres. The Veterans' Land Act provided financial funding for the construction of affordable prefab but permanent single-family homes and assisted returning veterans in purchasing the finished dwelling with a minimum down payment. The name "Victory Housing" concisely reflects both the civilian and military families who initially lived in these communities, also known by the postwar appellation "Veterans' Villages," that remain today visible in nearly every major town and city not only in Ontario, but throughout Canada.

Prefabricated and assembled on site by local builders and contractors, Victory Houses were available in several basic models with minor options. The most popular model, with steep roof, shallow eaves, small sash windows and clapboard exterior finish, is stylistically reminiscent of a simplified Cape Cod Colonial. Another model with a gable roof of lower profile and the optional three-part picture window provided a much more "modern" look to the house. Both centre- and side-hall plans were available, and, while clapboards were the favoured exterior finish, composite shingles, stucco, or brick veneer were also used. A small open entrance porch with thin trellislike supports was also available.

The compactness and neatness of the exterior appearance are a direct reflection of the efficiently arranged interiors. For instance, in order to minimize costs, dormers were excluded; the upper-floor rooms were lighted by windows at each gable end and serviced by a staircase that closely followed the slope of the roof.

Victory Housing (1940-1950)

Characteristic of Victory Housing are simplicity of form and lack of decorative enrichments. Individually these houses are not prime examples of high or academic style, but collectively they present to the public view a unique streetscape. In spite of numerous subsequent renovations and modifications to the original designs, their contextual value remains and their association with the war effort is reinforced by such street names as Churchill, Lancaster and even Victory Crescent.

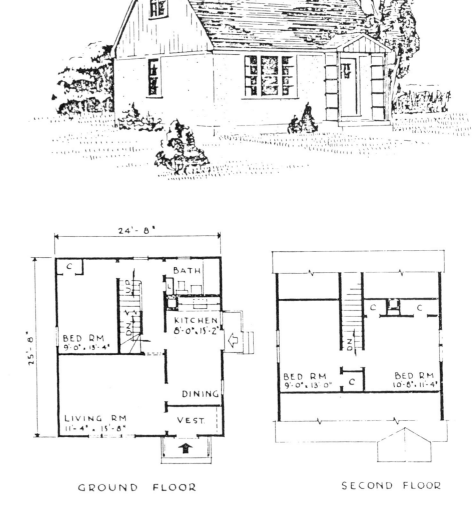

24—1
This VLA-0-9 model was one of the more popular plans available after the war. The second floor and a plate-glass picture window were available options. (Picture Collection, Public Archives of Canada)

24—2

24—3

A typical streetscape of Victory Houses in Peterborough, taken shortly after completion in 1943. Note the simple form without roof dormers, the traditional multipaned sash windows paired in the gable end and the small overdoor porch with latticelike supports for a Victory rose arbor. Built without basements and heated with a single stove, these houses were originally intended for temporary use. The metal stove chimney is visible rising from the rear roof slope. (Picture Collection, Public Archives of Canada)

24—4

Many of the early Victory Houses were modernized into permanent accommodation toward the end of the war. The property on the extreme left is one of the few that has not only retained the simple Cape Cod Colonial form but also many of the original details. Note the similarity of this house with the Peterborough illustration of 1943. (Windsor)

Victory Housing (1940-1950)

24—5
A streetscape of Victory Houses much altered in fenestration and exterior finishes, but by avoiding the addition of projecting roof dormers they retain the basic plain and compact form of their original appearance. (Thunder Bay)

24—6
Victory Houses were often planned in communities with crescents and cul de sacs. Note the smaller one-storey house with ventilator in the gable end. (Etobicoke)

24—7
The unpainted aluminum siding of this Victory House is rare today, but may have been an expedient extension of the market of a nearby factory that produced airplanes. Sash windows with two-over-two horizontal panes were an option to veterans who preferred a modern look. (Sault Ste. Marie)

24–8
Intentionally or not, this "street" of Victory Houses is distinctive in that the front yards are free of motorized vehicles. (Smiths Falls)

24–9
Rather than traditional clapboards, this Victory House, typical of the larger permanent house built for returning veterans, has composite shingle siding and a large three-part picture window. (Thunder Bay)

Chapter 25 '50s Contempo (1945-65)

Sarnia

Postwar contemporary design, simply termed '50s Contempo, reflects the optimism shared by many architects during this period of economic recovery and building boom. Of course, this style follows the principles of Modernism of the previous decades: functionalism, open space planning, the curtain wall, experimentation with new materials and forms and the strict avoidance of historicism.

Often the most striking feature of the Contempo style is the long linear roof, whose pitch, never steep, always approaches the horizontal. An absolutely flat roof is popular, but other more innovative profiles include shallow arches or vaults, sweeping slopes and the "butterfly" or inverted winglike form. These roofs are often continued well beyond the walls, exposing widely spaced steel or timber beams, as well as creating a cover for open patios, decks and carports. When needed, these overhanging roofs are supported by extending one supporting wall, or by thin metal columns or posts.

The static, Cubist compositions of the earlier prewar International style with their monochromatic wall finishes and small windows are now more dynamic, with varied materials and colour. Contempo designs are never enriched by adding historical detail but by varying materials and finishes, such as brick and stone with wood and metal siding. Façades are often highlighted with bright primary colours, red, blue, yellow and green, selectively applied on doors, window aprons and nonstructural curtain walls or panels. Colours are also seen on abstract mosaics and in stained-glass windows. A three-dimensional quality is heightened by contrasting a solid wall surface with large expanses of transparent glass. Large panes or sheets of plate glass (insulated thermopaned glass was not common until the 1970s) provide prototypes for the "picture window" motif seen on vernacular modern subdivision "ranch"-type houses. Smaller windows placed according to interior functional requirements slide, tilt or swing to open. A clerestory band of windows located high along a wall lights and ventilates an interior without sacrificing privacy. Large floor-to-ceiling glass doors slide open onto gardens and private courtyards. The main entrance often consists of a brightly coloured wood or metal door flanked by an equally large light to one side, with a smaller transom light above. At times the entrance façade of a house will have an emphatic one-storey elevation to one side, while the other half of the façade will have two storeys. This resulting asymmetrical split-level composition with the entrance off centre, bridging the levels, is the twentieth century's popular response to the traditional nineteenth century storey-and-a-half house. This split-level arrangement was quickly adopted as a standard suburban housing form where builders added on numerous stylistic references, including Colonial and Tudor.

Walter Gropius, who had worked briefly in England before going to the United States, continued to be influential as a teacher and practitioner. While at Harvard, Gropius explored the cooperative team approach to project design that resulted in buildings with industrial or high-tech qualities but, in contrast to the linear vertical thrust of the Miesian International style, were varied in composition and marked by a layering of grids with strong horizontal accents, including exterior balconies and railings. Le Corbusier, who worked more independently but was also a champion of experimentation, preferred an informal complexity of forms and textures. His Swiss Pavilion, 1930-32, University of Paris, France, used a long rectangular block as a backdrop to another vertical block. Different parts reflecting different functional uses were variously repeated with different materials and forms throughout Ontario, most notably for city hall and civic centres, such as ones in Hamilton, Ottawa, Windsor, and, most recently, in the Post-Modern Mississauga Civic Centre.

25—1
Derived from such Modernist monuments as the Swiss Pavilion, 1930-32, at the University of Paris, France, by Le Corbusier, this building shares with the Early International style a Cubist composition. (City Hall, Windsor)

25–2
In order to maximize passive solar heating, Contempo-style buildings were often designed with floor-to-ceiling windows having a southern exposure. Note, also, the hopperlike tilting transom windows, sun-screen trellis and clerestory windows lighting the attached garage wing. (St. Catharines)

25–3
A continuous single-slope shed roof with carport distinguish this house. (Etobicoke)

25-4

The following represent early variations
of the Contempo style built in the
postwar cooperative community of
Fairhaven Way. (Ottawa)

25-5
An asymmetrical balance of windows
against a Cubist form. (Fairhaven Way,
Ottawa)

'50s Contempo (1945-1965)

Marcel Breuer, who before going to the United States had worked with Gropius at the Bauhaus, is noted for imbuing contemporary designs with a more personable, down-to-earth, even rustic version of Modernism that is most appropriate to the '50s Contempo style. By integrating colour and texture with compatible, regionally available materials instead of accepting highly finished industrialized products, Breuer and Gropius in association with the Architects' Collaborative in Massachusetts, softened the monochromatic Bauhaus-derivative Cubist compositions and enlivened the Miesian steel-and-glass models.

Responding to the need for practical "modern"-inspired contemporary homes in the Ottawa area, a group, whose professional backgrounds included engineering and architecture, established the community known as Fairhaven Way. Individually designed homes utilizing ready-made standard building materials were economically constructed with communal assistance. Today Fairhaven Way possesses several early examples of excellent '50s Contempo-style houses, still in their wooded setting and some still occupied by their original designer-builder-owners. Fairhaven Way represents a Canadian application of Modernist design concepts tempered with 1950 contemporary materials and forms, very much following Gropius's and Breuer's cooperative team approach to the sensitive integration of regional materials.

25–6
A butterfly roof. (Fairhaven Way, Ottawa)

25—7
A split-level plan with asymmetrical three-sloped shed roof. (Fairhaven Way)

25—8
The lightness of the opened roof and exposed beams of the carport stands in contrast to the more solid-appearing walls and the rough stonework of the massive chimney. (Fairhaven Way, Ottawa)

25—9
Brick supporting walls combined with timber construction are highlighted by a large studio or stair hall window comprised of a grid of individual square panes. (Fairhaven Way, Ottawa)

25–10
Note the gridlike grouping of medium-sized panes to create a large window in this stone and wood Contempo style. (Georgetown)

25–11
A vernacular interpretation of Contempo-style materials and forms is evident in this flat-roof composition with stone, brick and wood finishes. Note the typical single door flanked by a large single-paned sidelight. (Sudbury)

25–12
The asymmetrical split-level composition with shallow-pitched, double-sloped roof was a popular plan. Exposed roof rafters, open carport, freestanding garden-implement shed, brightly coloured panels, painted wood siding and large-paned windows are very characteristic of the academic Contempo style. (Sault Ste. Marie)

25–13
In this case the Contempo style, characterized by strong horizontal lines, is reminiscent of the California Bungalow or ranch style. Note, also, the wide chimney on a cross axis, the thin metal columns supporting the continuous roof purlins and the placement of a skylight over the side door. (Thunder Bay)

25–14
This vernacular Contempo example, slightly modern yet traditional, assumes the basic form of many suburban "bungalow" or "ranch"-style homes. (London)

25–15
The vernacular Contempo-style house is characterized by a traditional gable roof, undersized Colonial shutters on the smaller window to the right and extra diagonal bracing for the cantilevered garage roof. (Sault Ste. Marie)

The Contempo style is often distinguished by low-pitched, shallow rooflines having if not always practical at least innovative profiles, as seen in the following examples:

25–16
Split-level roof reflects interior floor plan. (Ottawa)

25—17
Residential asymmetrical double slope.
(Thunder Bay)

25—18
Commercial asymmetrical double slope.
(Matheson)

25—19
Butterfly or inverted gable. (Strathroy)

25−20
Vaulted. (Guelph)

25−21
Conical. (London)

25—22
Winglike. (Windsor)

25—23
Tentlike festival roof. (Pembroke)

'50s Contempo (1945-1965)

And as in traditional styles, the entrance porticos announce the style:

25—24
Tapered concrete "pilotis" support a wavelike canopy. (Burlington)

25—25
Colourful mosaic-finished columns support this elongated "W" canopy. (Hamilton)

Chapter 26 **Brutalism (1960-1970)**

Brantford

As a concept, Brutalism, also known as "Neo or New Brutalism," was largely formulated by the English architects Peter and Alison Smithson in the early 1950s in response to what they perceived as the inadequacies of the International style. The historian Reyner Banham did much to document the development of the movement in his 1966 publication *New Brutalism*. Followers of Brutalism believed that modern architects of the time had failed to realize the true potential of the machine ethic and that their machine-for-living boxes lacked a personal or human component. The Brutalists bemoaned the anonymous emotionless glass-curtain wall that was then being rapidly applied all over London. Utilizing machine-produced materials in their "natural or as found" condition, the Brutalists hoped to satisfy human requirements through a varied composition of differing forms, shapes and textures.

Brutalist architecture also owes much to the Expressionist post-war work of Le Corbusier, such as his Dominican Monastery at La Tourette (1957-60) and the Unité d'habitation (1947-52), where he used *béton brut*, a concrete whose naturally textured surface is left as found after the wooden form work is removed. If the resulting surface was rough, uneven or oddly textured, so be it. Although materials were to be left "as found," with practice, architects learned to control the finishes by selecting appropriate materials for the form work. Also characteristic of this style was the exposure of the mechanical systems to public view. Visible heating ducts, plumbing pipes and electrical conduits along walls and ceilings of the interiors combined with the stark use of new materials became known in the 1980s as the decorative High Tech style.

In contrast to the sleek and highly finished buildings of the Miesian International or the colouristic '50s Contempo style, Brutalist buildings, relying on load-bearing walls, monochromatic tones and highly textured surfaces tend to appear massive and visually ponderous. Brutalists favoured concrete walls and at times brick. When steel and glass are used they never have the appearance of the thin nonload-bearing curtain wall. Rugged-looking walls may be windowless or at other times pierced by randomly placed apertures of various geometric shapes. Generally, windows are solid sheets of insulated glass with few if any provisions for opening, since interior spaces could be climatically controlled and

Brutalism (1960-1970)

seasonally adjusted. Brutalist buildings are complex in plan, not a translucent steel-and-glass box but a series of projecting and receding concrete forms of varying height, whose walls may be inclined or battered and cut at odd angles. With load-bearing walls, irregular massing and broken roofline, a comparison with the nineteenth century picturesque is tempting, but, like other proponents of "modern" architecture, the Brutalists avoid historically derived details and are thoroughly modern in material and technology.

In Ontario, Brutalism was popular for schools, offices and government buildings for a brief period. The Brantford City Hall Complex, 1964, by Michael Kopsa, architect, is very characteristic. A complex plan, a variety of forms and an irregular outline are finished with textured concrete or *béton brut*. Each exterior shape or part of the structure reflects a possible change in interior use or function. Stairs are located in rounded towers lighted on the opposing side by a single vertical ground-to-roof window. Projecting boxlike sun visors or screens frame individual office windows and function as protection against sun and rain. Huge windowless expanses of wall space enclose interior areas that may be artificially lighted with a combination of skylights and inner courtyards. Constructed at the end of Brutalism's short tenure is the Robarts Research Library, University of Toronto (Warner, Burns, Toan and Lunde with Mathers and Haldenby, 1968-73), with its emphatic vertical articulation of towers and ribs that may be likened to Gothic cathedrals, though the materials, finishes and massive composition are handled in typically Brutalist fashion.

Typical of Brutalism are the complex plan, variety of forms and irregular outline, with a textured concrete or béton brut finish, as illustrated in the Brantford City Hall Complex, 1964, Michael Kopsa, architect. Noteworthy features include:
- *battered windowless walls*
- *round-ended stair towers*
- *tall vertical window openings*
- *textures of wood form work left exposed*
- *projecting boxlike screens or visors*
- *horizontal joints of form work*
- *separate masses or blocks distinguishing interior functions*

26–1

26-2

26-3

26-4

26—5
*John P. Robarts Research Library, 1968-73, Warner, Burns, Toan and Lunde
with Mathers and Haldenby. Noteworthy features include:*
– monumental windowless walls
– béton brut concrete finishes
– massive buttresslike towers
– skeletal piers forming vertical shafts
– elevatorlike polygonal projecting bays
– narrow vertical windows
– extending polygonal sides forming recessed lightwell

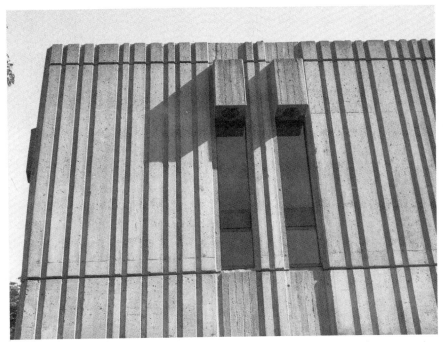

26—6
This Brutalist wall is characterized by wooden planks of random widths arranged to create deep vertical grooves or channels. The projecting blocklike window lintel provides cover for a recessed light. (Central Technical School Annex, Toronto).

26—7
Representative of the later phase of Brutalism, the desired textures of this wall become highly manipulated or overdesigned. The diagonal grooves against the battered wall with a concrete composition or aggregate consisting of a high proportion of large stones, approaching a "pebble dash" finish, is not a result of "as found" manufactured materials but has been expressly added to the design process. (Pumping Station, Windsor)

Brutalism (1960-1970)

26—8
Béton brut *or textured concrete is honestly expressed in this residential design, where the vertical board forms allude to a traditional plank fence and wall siding, while the second storey is treated with horizontal board forms complementing the long band of windows and the flat linear roof. In any other material, the shape and composition of this house, however late in date, might very well have been described as Prarie or International in style. (Toronto)*

26—9
An eclectic and minimal mix of International curtain wall with Brutalist structure results in an expression of vernacular constructivism. (Dundas)

26—10
A Brutalist exercise in concrete and geometry stands apart from its associated Miesian International-style office tower. (City Hall, North Bay)

26—11
A cantilevered terrace level separates the multifaceted geometry of the upper floors from the pedestrian scaled street level. (Toronto)

Chapter 27 Post-Modern (1970-present)

Mississauga

What followed the 1960s were for the most part variations on the theme of Modernism and the International style, and was known variously as Decorated Modern, Formalism, High Tech or simply Late Modern. However, during this period one group, led primarily by the American architect Robert Venturi, was exploring different avenues of expression that were most notable for their very decisive anti-Modern characteristics. Redirecting the mainstream of architectural practice, Post-Modern designs are marked by recognizable architectural forms and details drawn from a variety of historical styles, from ancient Greece through nineteenth century eclecticism to present-day twentieth century automobile-oriented vernacular. Chief among these historicisms is the return of the principal façade distinguished by an identifiable main entrance. Applied decorative ornament, usually Classical in origin, including robust mouldings and roof cornices, is also once again popular, as are polychromatic finishes, such as coloured brickwork and painted surfaces. Post-Modern designs also exhibit a strong contextual quality reflecting regional architectural characteristics: for example, a Colonial window, a gable roof and dichromatic brickwork. Since the International style and what was then "modern" has now become part of history, Post-Modern also includes features that are reminiscent of the immediate "modern" past. Thus, it would be acceptable to use a curtain wall of glass along with Classical pediments and columns.

Venturi's landmark book, *Complexity and Contradiction in Architecture*, 1966, was the first systematic examination of the inadequacies of Modernism in general and the stereotypical International style's steel-and-glass box in particular. Based upon a restructuring of numerous design factors that had been largely ignored by the previous generation of Modernists, Venturi urged his readers to look at, and rethink architecture by learning from the past, respecting the context of the existing environment and understanding regional and vernacular characteristics.

Post-Modernists look to history for recognizable and symbolic motifs and forms. Modernists had sought for an ideal or perfect form: Post-Modernists prefer to blend or harmonize new construction with vernacular and regional traits. In Post-Modern terms, vernacular includes ordinary utilitarian twentieth century buildings and structures that we all too often dismiss from our daily vision: all those auto-oriented service buildings such as car washes, drive-in convenience stores, dry cleaners, banks, fast-food outlets and strip plazas, with their associated neon signage and symbolism. Modernists believed that "form follows function" and that "less is more"! Post-Modernists have rethought function to incorporate personal tastes and group aesthetics as legitimate design factors and have restructured architecture to be complicated, layered with ambiguous or symbolic meanings, thus becoming representative of a pluralistic and multicultural society.

27–1
An ambiguous combination of vernacular forms with a hint of decorative Classicism often highlights Post-Modern designs. In this instance, the gable roof with one slope extended downward is reminiscent not only of the vernacular salt-box house shape of the early nineteenth century, but at the same time may be seen as an exaggerated gable from a Queen Anne style house. In Classical tradition the cut-out arch of the gable is perfectly balanced by the projecting half-round bay below, a popular form on some high style Neoclassical buildings. The uniform brick-wall construction accentuated with lattice trim and coloured vergeboard banding are all decoratively applied in contradiction to the principles of the modern nonhistorical styles of the past fifty years. (Markham Library, Phillip Carter, architect)

The architectural critic Charles Jencks, in his *Language of Post-Modern Architecture*, 1977, has further elaborated on Venturi's ideas, defining several Post-Modern directions that architects from around the world have been developing: "Radical Eclecticism," "Neovernacular," "Straight Revivalism" and the ultimate synthesis "Post-Modern Classicism," which places a strong emphasis on the symbolic and allegorical use of Classical motifs, particularly in public architectural design.

Venturi's observations and practice, combined with Jencks's analysis and definitions, have released a new generation of architects from past restrictions, opening "new-old" doors to explore on a broader, inclusive and more general basis. No doubt new discoveries will occur, experimentation will continue and further interpretations will be made as architects continue to explore the new age of electronic technology and computer-assisted architecture.

For Ontario architect Phillip Carter, Post-Modern represents a search of our colonial roots for qualities of old buildings that have relevance in today's architecture. This historical interest, combined with the lessons learned from Modernism, results in designs characterized by an eclectic array of simplified nineteenth century forms, such as broad gables and round-headed windows; a sparse application of minimalized or freely adapted Classical elements, including columns, pediments and mouldings; and a "Modernist" framework with large expanses of industrial-looking windows or a ribbon or banding of smaller casement-type windows. Carter's Markham Library, 1982, is one such recent attempt to synthesize Historicism with Modernism.

27–2
In typical Post-Modern language the pediment is stretched beyond its traditional proportions, creating an affinity more with the vernacular false or boomtown fronts of Ontario than with temples of ancient Greece. A cutout lunette and stone banding intensify the superficial Classical symbolism of this commercial strip-plaza. (Mississauga)

27–3
A Romanesque Revival round arch with exaggerated impost returns is executed with brick veneer in the Post-Modernist style. (Bowmanville)

27–4
Attempts at relieving the monotony of steel-framed glass boxes with a variety of nonhistorical add-on decorative finishes, including patterned steel screens, contoured concrete panels, repetitive but small or oddly shaped windows and colourful sculptural motifs, are best referred to as Decorated Modern. (Guelph)

247

Post-Modern (1970-present)

27-5
Returning to the "streamlining" effect of the earlier Art Moderne style results in a very appropriate symbol for this Post-Modern building serving as a harbour-marina facility. (Sarnia)

27-6
The Post-Modernist's return to history and controlled materials is evidenced by this recent high-rise building with instant pre-aged metal siding imitating what the Brutalists had desired to achieve "naturally." (Toronto)

27—7
Post-Modernists accept the nonhistorical modern styles of the past fifty years as history and therefore can emulate "Modernist" elements as readily as Classical ones. Of particular note on this undecorated Cubistic Post-Modern frontispiece are steel-framed corner windows and a concrete "piloti" or column in opposition to a brick-veneered pier. (Toronto)

27—8
This Late Modern office building, with reflective glass and polished-stone framing, is provided a Post-Modern form with a drumlike centre flanked by steplike wings. (Markham)

Post-Modern (1970-present)

27–9
The historical precedents are not so obvious or directly copied, but rather imaginatively abstracted into a unique pastiche of textures and forms. (London)

27–10
Historical precedents are clearly expressed in details, such as the end-wall chimney, arched gable-end windows and rock-faced stone banding. (Brampton)

27–11
Traditional fire station with its tall tower is highlighted with dichromatic banding typical of the nineteenth century vernacular. (Markham)

Selected
further reading

Adamson, Anthony. *The Gaiety of Gables, Ontario's Architectural Folk Art.* Toronto: McClelland and Stewart, 1974.

Angus, Margaret. *The Old Stones of Kingston, Its Buildings before 1867.* Toronto: University of Toronto Press, 1966.

Arthur Eric. *Toronto, No Mean City.* Toronto: University of Toronto Press, third edition, 1986.

Beckman, Margaret, Stephan Langmead and John Black. *The Best Gift: A Record of the Carnegie Libraries in Ontario.* Toronto: Dundurn Press, 1984

Bernstein, William and Ruth Crawker. *Contemporary Canadian Architecture.* Toronto: Fitzhenry and Whiteside, 1982.

Blake, Verschoyle Benson and Ralph Greenhill. *Rural Ontario.* Toronto: University of Toronto, 1969.

Blumenson, John J-G. *Identifying American Architecture: A Pictorial Guide to Styles and Terms, 1600-1945.* Nashville: American Association for State and Local History, 1977.

Brooks, H. Allen. *Prairie School Architecture.* Toronto: University of Toronto Press, 1975.

Brosseau, Mathilde. *Gothic Revival Architecture. Canadian Historic Sites,* Occasional Papers in Archaeology and History, No. 25. Ottawa: Parks Canada, 1980.

Cameron, Christina and Janet Wright. *Second Empire Style in Canadian Architecture. Canadian Historic Sites,* Occasional Papers in Archaeology and History, No. 24. Ottawa: Parks Canada, 1980.

Clerk, Nathalie. *Palladian Style in Canadian Architecture. Studies in Archaeology, Architecture and History.* Ottawa: Parks Canada, 1984.

Cruickshank, Tom and Peter John Stokes. *The Settler's Dream, A Pictorial History of the Older Buildings of Prince Edward County.* Picton: Corporation of the County of Prince Edward, 1984.

Dendy, William. *Lost Toronto.* Toronto: Oxford University Press, 1978.

_____ *Toronto Observed.* Don Mills: Oxford University Press, 1986.

Gowans, Alan. *Building Canada: An Architectural History of Canadian Life.* Toronto: Oxford University Press, 1966.

_____ *The Comfortable House: North American Suburban Architecture, 1890-1930.* Cambridge: MIT Press, 1986.

Greenhill, Ralph, Ken Macpherson and Douglas Richardson. *Ontario Towns.* Ottawa: Oberon, 1974.

Hitchcock, Henry-Russell and Philip Johnson. *The International Style.* New York: W.W. Norton, 1966.

Hubka, Thomas C. *Big House, Little House, Back House, Barn: the Connected Farm Buildings of New England.* Hanover: University Press of New England, 1984.

Humphreys, Barbara, and Meredith Sykes. *The Buildings of Canada: A Guide to Pre-20th Century Styles in Houses, Churches, and Other Structures.* Montreal: The Reader's Digest Association, 1974.

Hunt, Geoffrey. *John M. Lyle: Toward a Canadian Architecture.* Kingston: Agnes Etherington Art Centre, Queen's University, 1982.

Hutchins, Nigel. *Restoring Old Houses.* Toronto: Van Nostrand Reinhold Ltd., 1980.

Kalman, Harold and John Roaf. *Exploring Ottawa.* Toronto: University of Toronto Press, 1983.

Leaning, John and Lyette Fortin. *Our Architectural Ancestry.* Ottawa: Haig and Haig Publishing Co., n.d.

MacRae, Marion and Anthony Adamson. *The Ancestral Roof: Domestic Architecture of Upper Canada.* Toronto: Clarke Irwin, 1963.

_____ *Hallowed Walls: Church Architecture of Upper Canada.* Toronto: Clarke Irwin, 1975.

_____ *Cornerstones of Order: Courthouses and Town Halls of Ontario, 1784-1914.* Toronto: Clarke Irwin, 1983.

McAlester, Virginia and Lee. *A Field Guide to American Houses.* New York: Alfred Knopf, 1984.

McHugh, Patricia. *Toronto Architecture: A City Guide.* Toronto: Mercury Books, 1985.

Maitland, Leslie. *Palladian Style in Canadian Architecture. Studies in Archaeology, Architecture and History.* Ottawa: Parks Canada, 1984.

Noble, Allen G. *Wood, Brick and Stone: The North American Settlement Landscape,* Volume 1: Houses. Amherst: University of Massachusettes Press, 1984.

Otto, Stephan A. and Richard M. Dumbrille. *Maitland: A Very Neat Village Indeed.* Erin: Boston Mills Press, 1985.

Peacock, David and Suzanne. *Old Oakville.* Willowdale: White/Hounslow Productions, 1979.

Popeliers, John et al. *What Style Is It: A Guide to American Architecture.* Washington, D.C.: The Preservation Press, 1983.

Rempel, John I. *Building with Wood.* Toronto: University of Toronto Press, 1972.

Rifkind, Carole. *A Field Guide to American Architecture.* Scarborough: New American Library, 1980.

Stokes, Peter John. *Old Niagara-on-the-Lake.* Toronto: University of Toronto Press, 1971.

Stokes, Peter John, Tom Cruickshank and Robert Heaslip. *Rogues Hollow: The Story of the Village of Newburgh, Ontario through Its Buildings.* Toronto: The Architectural Conservancy of Ontario, 1983.

Tausky, Nancy A. and Lynne DiStefano. *Victorian Architecture in London and Southwestern Ontario.* Toronto: University of Toronto Press, 1986.

Whiffen, Marcus. *American Architecture Since 1780: A Guide to The Styles.* Cambridge: MIT Press, 1969.

Whiffen, Marcus and Frederick Koeper. *American Architecture, 1607-1976.* London: Routledge and Kegan Paul, 1981.

Wright, Janet. *Architecture of the Picturesque in Canada. Studies in Archaeology, Architecture and History.* Ottawa: Parks Canada, 1984.

Index

255